Online Sales Funnels

A Beginners Guide To Customer Growth

Copyright © Prabinder Sahonta, 2021

All rights reserved. No part of this book may be reproduced in any form on by an electronic or mechanical means, including information storage and retrieval systems, without permission in writing from the publisher, except by a reviewer who may quote brief passages in a review.

First paperback edition February 2021

Cover illustration by messyspace.uk

ISBN: 979-8-7041-9199-5 (paperback)

Published by SliikFunnels

www.sliikfunnels.com

"To my late mother, for my inspiration, drive, fight and strength. And to my father, for saving me and without whom, none of this would be possible."

Table of Contents

1.0 INTRODUCTION 5

2.0 AN INSIGHT IN DIGITAL MARKETING 7

    2.1 A BRIEF HISTORY...8

    2.2 SELLING ONLINE 10

    2.3 EVOLUTION 16

3.0 INTRODUCING WEB ANALYTICS AND FUNNELS 18

    3.1 A QUICK FUNNEL SETUP 22

4.0 MAPPING THE BUYER'S JOURNEY 26

5.0 SALES FUNNELS: A COMPREHENSIVE GUIDE 29

    5.1 BACKGROUND 29

    5.2 WINTER PARKA – A SALES FUNNEL STORY 29

    5.3 JOURNEY BY METHOD 31

    5.4 BENEFITS OF THE SALES FUNNEL 36

    5.5 FUNNEL ANALYSIS 37

    5.6 B2B AND B2C FUNNELS 39

    5.7 COSTS & CONVERSIONS..40

    5.8 MARKETING VS SALES 42

    5.9 NON-LINEAR FUNNELS 43

    5.10 FLIPPING THE FUNNEL 45

6.0 THE ONLINE SALES FUNNEL 47

    6.1 THE FUNNEL IS EVOLVING 47

    6.2 THE NEW ONLINE MODEL 48

    6.3 ONLINE FUNNEL TYPES...50

        6.3.1 The Hourglass Online Funnel...50

        6.3.2 Looping Online Funnel 51

        6.3.3 Micro-Moments Online Funnel 52

7.0 PLUGGING THE LEAK 53

   7.1 METRICS 53

      7.1.1 Key Performance Indicators 54

      7.1.2 More Than The Metrics 57

   7.2 Search Engine Optimisation (SEO) 58

   7.3 Retargeting 59

   7.4 Live Chat 59

   7.5 Artificial Intelligence (AI) & Machine Learning 60

   7.6 A Quick Reference Guide 62

   7.7 Adapt To Survive 63

8.0 SALES FUNNEL SOFTWARE 64

9.0 WRAP UP 69

10.0 APPENDICES 70

   Appendix II Funnel Objectives 71

   Appendix III Common & Successful Funnel Types 72

   Appendix IV Funnel Categories 73

   Appendix V Real-World Successful Funnels 75

GLOSSARY 77

1.0 INTRODUCTION

Convinced by marketing spiel touting six figure sum sales within a year and customer testimonials stating they have gone from nothing to being zillionaires, you have decided to take the plunge and invest in the world of e-commerce. However driving traffic to your site is proving harder than you thought. Your ticking over with meagre results and cannot comprehend why, even with all that advertising cash you have splurged on Zuckerberg's cash cow.

For that matter it seems like every year there are news report of another record breaking profit from the likes of Amazon, Alibaba and Rakuten. Posting sales figures that run into the hundreds of millions, if not billions. All on the back of an e-commerce model that was unfathomable only two decades ago. Exactly how do such online enterprises consistently acquire leads that convert into profitable sales? What are the tools and techniques that underpin such success, and how accessible are they to the budding entrepreneur? All of these are burning questions in the minds of online entrepreneurs, and digital marketing proffers the solutions to them.

In the last decades, online sales and digital marketing were all but alien concepts to many. In recent times, they have taken a major stake in the world economy and marketplace with bricks and mortar giving way to online stores and billboards to website banners. Combined with a business model that has the ability to directly harness and target customers by employing the multitude of innovations the internet provides. It is therefore apparent that businesses that are thriving in the current marketplace, are those that have adapted to new paradigm of e-commerce, online advertising and web analytics.

Furthermore, in recent years, the online sales funnel has stood out as a key factor in driving growth.

With new software that makes it more accessible, no need for coding or technical know-how. The online sales funnel affords a business opportunity to creatively advance, probing their target markets more efficiently and effectively than traditional advertising and marketing. The digital marketplace has progressed rapidly over the years, and it will continue to do so, and an ever-increasing number of businesses like Rakuten, Ikea and Budweiser are transitioning to more analytical, insightful and interactive marketing campaigns with measurable success to show for it.

INTRODUCTION

We discuss the success and breakthrough of digital marketing, the advantages if offers you as a business owner and aspiring e-commerce guru. The subject matter is arguably a vast network comprised of several pillars, that can be overwhelming, even daunting for those navigating it themselves for the first time. This book steers you through the lens of one of its most significant pillars – the sales funnel. Using it as a conduit into digital marketing concepts, web analytics and ultimately customer growth. Providing an in-depth guide for successfully preparing a comprehensive digital marketing strategy using the sales funnel as it's focal point, traversing the many innovations the internet has to offer. Leading you through the following:

> "The subject matter is arguably a vast network comprised of several pillars, that can be overwhelming, even daunting for those navigating it themselves for the first time. This book steers you through the lens of one of its most significant pillars – the sales funnel."

- The fundamentals of Digital Marketing and Web Analytics.
- An in-depth analysis of the customer journey from prospect to advocate.
- Tips, tools and strategies for the each stage of the customer journey.
- A case study, an example of sales funnel theory in practice.
- An in-depth analysis of the online sales model, its evolution and how to adapt.
- Appendices – Lists of online funnel objectives, types and real world success stories.

All of which aimed at embedding your understanding and providing you the means to get started on your journey to increased online customer growth.

2.0 AN INSIGHT IN DIGITAL MARKETING

Advertising, when performed through digital means such as search engines, social media and e-mail, falls under the wider umbrella of digital marketing. As a process it transcends internet advertising and marketing, and includes display advertising, Search Engine Optimization (SEO) and Search Engine Marketing (SEM). The main objective and purpose of which is to increase brand awareness and promote sales by digital media means.

One of the demands of digital marketing is to take a novel and innovative approach to advertising, and aim to have a profound comprehension of customer needs, wants, and particularly behaviour. It requires in-depth analysis and quantification of marketing campaigns to ensure that the right offers and messages get to the right pool of customers, at the right time in exactly the right place. The advent of social media and the inherent need of humans to stay in touch with one another, has ensured that people are increasingly spending a great deal of time online. News websites, blogs, video streaming services, social media and the like, offer a plethora of opportunities for business to target prospective audiences with their product and services. Channelled through digital marketing, such prospects become aware, develop an interest, and ultimately act to purchase, becoming your customers.

The buying and selling process in the past did at times prove to be a strenuous and exhausting experience. Customers would have to visit stores in person to learn about products, services and price.

Taking guidance from family and friends, looking for that great recommendation. The process was not much easier for business owners either; their sphere of influence covered a few square miles, with a limited customer base.

> **"The marketing of products or services using digital channels to reach consumers. The key objective is to promote brands through various forms of digital media..."**
>
> *- Financial Times, Lexicon.*

With the internet and digital marketing, the buying and selling process is pretty much an instant affair, traversing continents and oceans. Any person or business can perform their own research, acquiring sufficient knowledge to make an comparative, informed decision on that next purchase.

Digital marketing helps consumers become invested in their purchase. Providing information that meets a need or problem and in turn, attempting to build a strong affinity with your brand. Business can chart the course of consumer behaviour, identify their interests, and extend that reach like never before. Digital marketing as a tool has transformed the science of advertising, offering business a greater degree of efficiency than ever.

CHAPTER 2 AN INSIGHT IN DIGITAL MARKETING

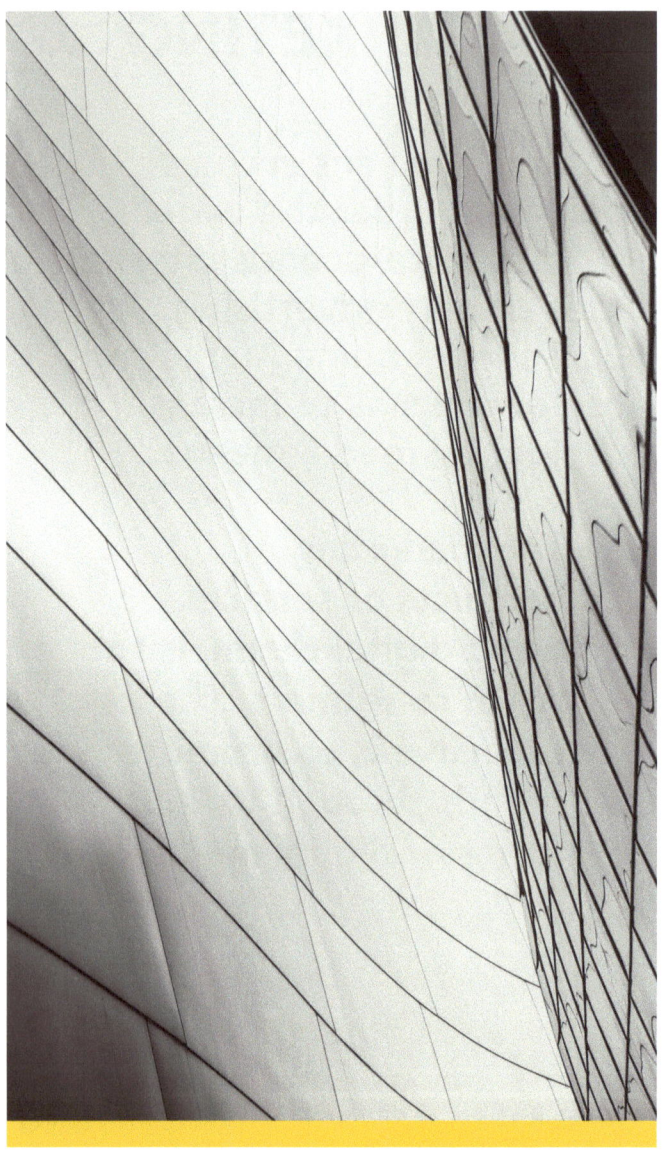

So, where does the online sales funnel figure in to all this? As a digital marketing tool it is useful for leads, conversion, cross selling, optimisation as well as many other benefits. As a business owner, it provides you with opportunities and advantages that traditional marketing cannot afford you. For example, behavioural targeting through distinct analysis patterns of your online consumers.

Regardless of what services or products you offer, digital marketing is indispensable tool in your arsenal for business growth. Having outpaced traditional marketing in terms of innovation and designed to reach a much larger pool of customers than the former ever could.

2.1 A BRIEF HISTORY

The origin of Digital Marketing as a form of consumer engagement can be traced back to the late 80s and the beginning of the 90s. As a term, it was first used in 1990, when people had just begun to access the internet, with the World Wide Web becoming widely available in 1991. Within five years, the number of internet users had skyrocketed to a whopping 16 million; it was the beginning of the online information era, and the first search engine, Archie, was born.

With the first clickable web-ad banner developed in 1994, and the launch of Yahoo! in 1995, Customer Relationship Management (CRM) tools became some of the chief investment areas for business growth. A technology used to manage interactions with customers and potential customers. In 1999, the electronic Customer Relationship Management (eCRM) was launched. Alongside the existing features of the CRM, eCRM incorporated internet integration and the capability to store information online. This was a breakthrough for business as they could now mange much larger volumes of data; the end of bulky and cumbersome customer management was rapidly approaching.

With the eCRM came new challenges: businesses amassed huge amounts of customer data but no clear indication of how to utilise it. Salesforce.com, the first Software as a Service (SaaS) company was developed to solve that problem. Creators of the marketing cloud software, they were able to assist businesses in consolidating consumer data storage with campaign tracking, community building, brand boosting and analytics. The marketing cloud software would later become a focal and reference point in marketing technology.

CHAPTER 2 AN INSIGHT IN DIGITAL MARKETING

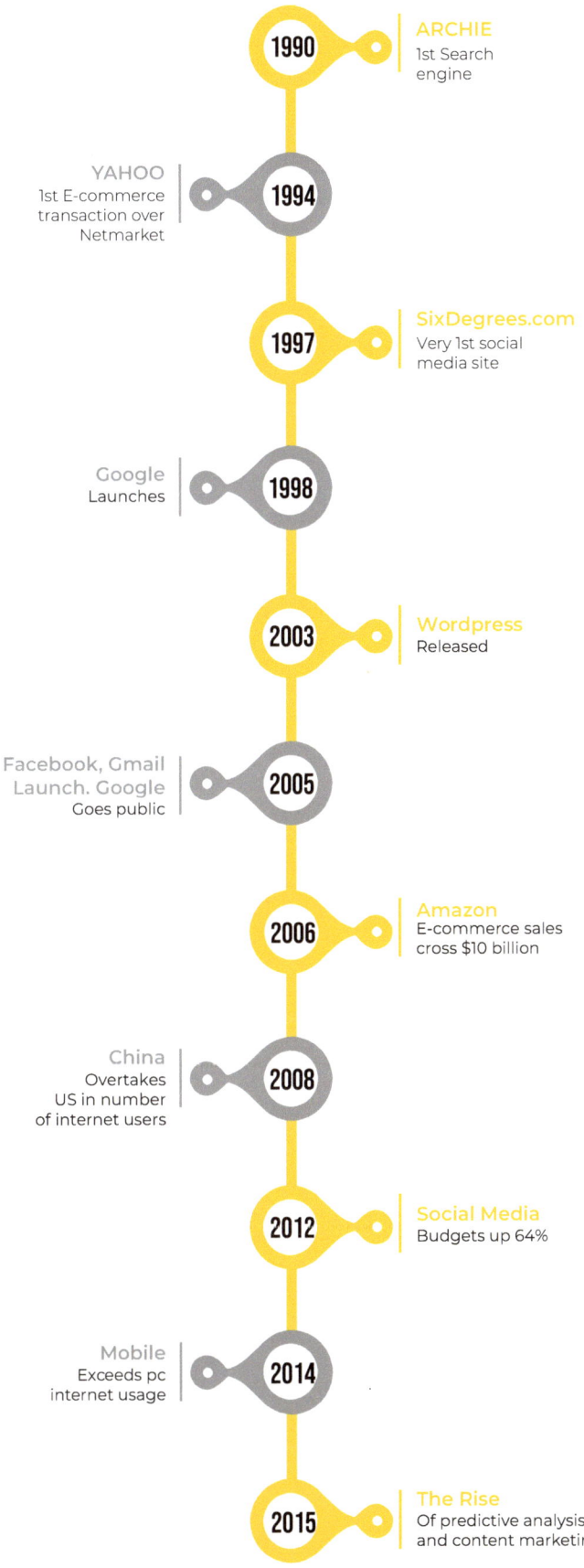

The 2000s dawned to see a change in behavioural norms of customers. Search engines like Yahoo and Google (developed in 1998) made customers actively begin searching for, and research products online before making final purchasing decisions. As a result business owners were thrown in a quandary, tried as much as they did, they could not quite grasp the psychology behind purchasing decisions. This problem remain unsolved until marketing automation platforms were introduced by companies like Act and Pardot. The platforms allowed business owners to partition the market and have a shot at multi-channel campaigns that would become the root of marketing analytics.

Social media platforms like Facebook (2004), YouTube (2005), Twitter (2006), and WhatsApp (2009), gained popularity in the late 2000s, birthing new marketing opportunities. The advent of the smartphones provided consumers quick, easy and affordable access to the internet. Delivering business another avenue down which they could to reach consumers through mobile optimised marketing.

The 2010s saw the biggest shift in consumer online transactions to date. Dependence on mobile phones for daily activities peaked. From making calls to sending videos, purchasing goods, and taking online courses, there was a mobile app for everything, and people spent increasingly more hours surfing the web on their smartphones. Furthermore, social media platforms became inundated with paid ads and promoted posts. Which began to account for a large percentage of the total revenue for their parent companies. This all resulted in a seismic shift in online marketing, targeting mobile and social.

Figure 2.1.1 – Digital marketing timeline

CHAPTER 2 AN INSIGHT IN DIGITAL MARKETING

Marketing campaign activity became more of an exact art, as opposed to an approximate one. Marketers gained the capability to channel campaigns directly to a targeted demographic. Vastly increasing the likelihood of translating campaigns into sales. Websites progressively became mobile optimised, as consumers proved more liable to purchase online when sites better fit their smartphone experience.

Lastly, messenger apps allowed a more personal and direct relationship between business and their customers. Content marketing such as Facebook stories, Pinterest ideas or Instagram influencer posts caused another change in the marketers' approach. Resulting in an increased focus in generating leads through content marketing.

2.2 SELLING ONLINE

As we dig deeper into models, tools and techniques for promoting online sales growth, it would be prudent to touch upon the basics of online selling and it's guiding principles.

Creating money online falls into three broad categories:

1. Selling your own product or services.
2. Monetising traffic.
3. Promoting affiliate product or services.

Product & Services

Creating your own products or services online can prove to be very lucrative and rewarding. Whilst it comes with its challenges, there is no substitute than having complete creative control over your product and it's direction. Having your own product to sell is not necessarily the only option, instead you could offer to become a reseller for a multitude of online companies, such as drop shipping through Shopify or selling internet domain services as a Big Commerce white label partner. Acting as a proxy and advocate, taking a share in the profits, mitigating your risk exposure with a proven product or service, with the caveat that you relinquish creative control and keep substantially less money.

Let's consider some product and service types that have proved to be popular for both selling and promoting original content:

- Information products: E.g. How-to-book or online course. Probably the easiest way to start selling online as the cost is relatively low. Almost anyone can develop informational content using desktop software and publish in formats such as .pdf or .epub.

- Audio: E.g. Podcasts. Recording equipment is readily accessible and cheap. Creating your own recorded products and promotional content has never been easier.

- Video: E.g. Promotional video. Every website can enhance the buyer's experience with a video, especially when you have a product for sale. Video has proven to be particularly effective online and cost of software and equipment has come down substantially over the years.

CHAPTER 2 AN INSIGHT IN DIGITAL MARKETING   11

Banner Advertising: Accomplished through an advertising client, displaying traditional banner ads on your sites. There are various ways in which this operates, the most common ones are listed below:

- *Cost Per Click (CPC):* As the name suggests, you are paid for each ad click at an agreed amount with the advertising client. For example, 5,000 clicks at 3 cents per click, for a total of $150.

- *Cost Per 1,000 Page Views (CPM):* An advertiser simply pays you in advance to showcase their ad on a page, in your website. This is based on an agreed number of times the ad is accessed by visitors.

- *Pay Per Call/Lead:* Payment is made for each call or lead generated as a result of the ad being displayed on your website. The caveat being calls need to be of an agreed quality.

- *Call Per Action (CPA):* The advertiser only pays once a sale is closed. In essence, this is similar to being in an affiliate program, as payment is only made upon a sale.

Monetising Traffic

It you're not selling your own products or running an affiliate program, it is still possible to make money simply from traffic to your site:

Google AdSense: A popular and vast network of advertising on the internet. Works by adding a small snippet of code provided by Google to your website. Ads then display based on the content your offering. Money is made each time an ad is clicked, the actual amount varies, as it depends on how much the advertiser has been willing to pay. However, Google do calculate ads that have the most potential of working on your site. What is imperative in this model is to have lots of pages and traffic for it to really make commercial sense. The idea here is to drive traffic to other sites, therefore selling your own products with AdSense is not recommended.

Promoting Affiliate Products or Services

Affiliate products and services are items that another party has created, delivered and supports. You receive payment in the form of sales commission, for promotion and a subsequent sale from your website. A website is not necessarily required, this can be a digital ad or even simply a link in an email. How it normally works is that the business provide what is known as an affiliate link or banner. Which you then promote in which ever method you choose.

CHAPTER 2 AN INSIGHT IN DIGITAL MARKETING

Note, you do not need to be a Fortune 500 company to run an affiliate program. As a business owner, you can very easily setup and run your own program. Giving away a share of your profit to channel more traffic into your funnel is a great way to grow that customer base.

The Buying Process

> **"A smooth buying process is critical, a poor one will prove to be detrimental to your business. Resulting in a loss of sales, customers and eventually reputation."**

All of which are easily and rapidly accomplished online through reviews, social media and consumer choice websites. A positive experience on the other hand, builds trust. A prospect feels content in handing over there hard earned money and more importantly, likely to come back. Let's look at the key parts of the process, together with tips to ensure customers have an encouraging experience.

Transaction Page: The page for entering contact and credit card information. This can be in one of two ways:

1. Shopping cart: Undoubtedly the most popular way to sell online and something you are already familiar with. The concept stems from the traditional shopping experience, where you would typically use a cart in a grocery store, selecting items from the shelf, adding them to your basket and then paying at the till. Online this scenario equates to an "Add To Cart" call to action (CTA), filling your virtual basket, leading to a Checkout page that acts as your till.

2. Custom form: Not all business are ideally suited to the shopping cart model. This is where the custom form comes in. Allowing you to create and customise any arrangement of product or service purchase. This does come with its limits, chiefly an altogether greater deal of effort in terms of development, support and subsequently cost. As opposed to using an out-of-the box shopping cart module.

The decision to go with either approach ultimately comes down to your business model, cost and turnaround time. Whilst a custom form order process will align perfectly with the buyer journey you envisaged, a shopping cart service will have you up and running a lot quicker and be cheaper to run.

The Merchant Account: Your payment transactions must be collected and tracked in some way. A customer needs to handover credit card details and then trust that you have the means to securely complete the transaction. Therefore your transaction page will be integrated with a merchant provider to accept payments by credit or debit cards, the most well-known being PayPal. However, there are other merchants available and would be wise to explore the costs and benefits of other providers. Cost permitting, you can also offer more than one provider. Giving the customer such options mitigates any loss of sale based on customer payment method preferences.

The Payment Gateway

The processor for the financial settlement of credit and debit card transactions. Ties your transaction page with your merchant account. Effectively this is the gatekeeper of your customer's payment data. Relaying the information from you, the merchant, to the acquirer (payment processing company) and issuing bank. The guiding principle here is to have this performed in the most secure way, using data encryption to protect against any threats to data. Popular vendors; PayPal, WePay, Authorize.net, Stripe.

Good Practice:

- Ensure the look and feel of your order page coincides with that of rest of the website. Otherwise users can lose trust in the purchase, after being confronted with an altogether different looking page requesting their payment details.

- Display the item description, quantity and price again on the order page. This affirms the users assumption of exactly what they are purchasing.

- Show ALL payment options. E.g., credit cards, PayPal etc.

- Do not include navigation buttons on the order page. This prevents the user from being drawn to exit the transaction.

- Custom "Thank You" page for each product or service purchase. This allows for a greater chance to cross-sell related products.

- Send automated emails or sequence of emails for a purchase. This affords you the capability of marketing other products, services or promotional offers.

- Ease of use: Ensure that adding and maintaining items in the shopping cart is easily done. Consider speed, simplicity and strong clear, clean "Add To Cart" CTA's.

- Consider using coupon codes. If your using an out-of-the box Shopping cart, then this should be one of the features it ships with. These enable you to run promotional campaigns and provides a clear indication of performance on such activity.

- Clearly display any registered adherence to data or financial compliance on your website. Such General Data Protection Regulation (GDPR), Payment Card Industry Security Standard (PCI DSS) or Secure Socket Layer (SSL) certificates.

- Provide the user with pre and post purchase support for the transaction, be that on the phone (preferably), live chat, email or order tracking. Again, builds trust with the visitor if they see that all this is available ahead of a purchase.

CHAPTER 2 AN INSIGHT IN DIGITAL MARKETING

Customer Questions

Handing over credit card details online is not a decision taken lightly by most people. In an age of data breaches and cybercrime, people will consciously or sub-consciously explore reasons to doubt you. All within a few minutes of taking a purchase decision. You therefore have those precious minutes to clearly answer any doubts that are circulating in their head. For that matter, you need to think about every possible question and have the answers clearly at hand. Through onsite pages such as sales, product, transaction, checkout, and in a transparent FAQ section. Here are sample of typical questions you may need to address:

How do I get what I ordered?

- Delivery method, a download link, pick up where? etc.

How long will it take to get what I ordered?

- Availability (in stock), estimated delivery duration.

Is this site secure?

- Display your security credentials.

How legitimate are you as a company?

- Use testimonials to build trust.

What will be done with my data after purchase?

- Assure data security and GDPR compliance.

How do I go about getting a refund?

- Clear return and refund policy or terms.

Should I expect more communication from you?

- In line with GDPR, clearly label any opt-in communication request.

Am I ordering the right product?

- Provide assurance the product is the right fit. E.g. "ideal if you have just launched your e-commerce business".

Is this best price?

- Inform the user you are best price for this product (ethically speaking, ensure this is genuinely the case).

Is this the end of the sales process?

- Clearly display to the buyer where they are in the sales process. Ending with an on-screen message when complete.

Upselling

> **Why not make it a large one for only $2 more?"**

– A typical upsell in a fast food restaurant, convincing someone to spend that little more during the checkout process. Online this is classically performed on the order confirmation page. Where the planned purchase is itemised together with an upsell product, demonstrating a saving or added value, if you only spend that little more. Normally, an unchecked item, that you simply tick to update your order. A popular tactic online that has been the staple of e-commerce platforms from inception.

Cross-selling

Conceptually similar to upselling, with the exception that the product being promoted during the order confirmation is related in some way to the purchase. E.g. Being pushed hosting services, when purchasing an internet domain on an Internet Services website. Consider it as promoting accessories to the purchase.

Cross-selling can equally be applied post purchase. In fact, it is arguably better to push the accessory after a purchase has been completed. If you know your audience well, you will know which the customers will prefer.

Back-end Selling

Getting visitors to your business in some guise, such as a subscribing to a newsletter or downloading a free e-book, proffers an opportunity to sell on the "back" of it. Essentially, this is an example of what is termed as *lead magnet* in marketing speak. Something we discuss comprehensively in oncoming chapters.

However, for now here are some further examples:

- A follow up promotion email, following a free sample.
- A meeting or phone call, following a registration for an event your hosting.
- Personalised promotional email, following a registered visitor interest your business.

Creating Your Own Affiliate Program

Ideally you have some experience in affiliate marketing ahead of running your own program. That experience will drive the advice and materials you provide your affiliates. As well as identifying what works, what does not work and refined promotional techniques. Regardless, even a relatively small affiliate program can have a moderate impact to your sales growth. When done well, that can quite easily grow to a substantial one. Let's explore the basic components to getting setup:

- An Affiliate Centre: A place for affiliates to manage their accounts. Obtain links, materials, check sales and scripts to promote.

- Payment Tracking System: Ideally you want a mechanised way of paying your affiliates on time. This will go a long way to building trust and keep your affiliates engaged and motivated.

There are numerous affiliate providers that package the above components, servicing both business owners and affiliate marketers. Popular ones among them are: Amazon Associates, CJ Affiliate and ShareASale.

As a business owner running an affiliate program you have some work to do:

- Attract affiliates. Get the word out your looking for affiliates, use your social media and business networks. The best people, are your customers. Loyal, advocates are ideal to approach.

- Training: When you onboard an affiliate, have a ready-made training program. Provide them the materials, such as links, banners, graphics, videos and copy. When the numbers are small, coach them with one-to-one sessions.

- Evaluate: Run a weekly or monthly conference call meeting, where your affiliates can ask questions to improve their numbers, you can provide updates and generally gauge performance. Keep it short and concise, otherwise people will fail to engage and drop off.

2.3 EVOLUTION

Together with the internet, digital marketing has come a long way since its inception over 30 years ago. From the first clickable web-ad banners in the 1990s, social media marketing in the 2000's to mobile optimised campaigns in the 2010's. What this has proved is that digital marketing growth and innovation go hand in hand with that of the internet and digital technology.

 As of 2020, there are approximately 4.66 billion internet users and 2.4 billion social networking users online at any one time.

A number that is expected to increase to 3.1 billion by 2021. Marketers have adapted to the new reality that is social media, like they did with video streaming and mobile. Whatever the innovation, marketers have learned to adapt and run with it. So what does the future hold for digital marketing?

In recent times it has been social networking and social media that have spearheaded the digital marketing revolution. Such as influencers on social media platforms, a $1billion industry, expected to double by 2021. Another seismic shift has been the relative ease with which consumers can now access, research, and review products. Consequently marketing is increasingly having to cater for a more informed prospect. As you will see in coming chapters, this has had a significant impact to how marketers approach their sales funnels, leads and campaign activity.

The advent of Artificial Intelligence (AI) in the marketing space, is possibly the most exciting one to watch:

 Artificial intelligence is the biggest commercial opportunity for companies, industries, and nations over the next few decades and will increase global GDP by up to 14% between now and 2030, which means that AI latecomers will find themselves at a serious competitive disadvantage within the next several years." [a]

For example auto-responding personalised emails, that stem from user behaviour analysis. In a similar vein AI digital advertising; analysing user information, such as gender, age, interests, and demographics to display tailored advertisements, measurably improving the performance of digital ads like never before.

CHAPTER 2 AN INSIGHT IN DIGITAL MARKETING

Managing the buyer's journey is the linchpin on which all this hangs. Working smarter and more efficiently through insightful analysis is key in unleashing the true benefits of marketing digitally. The transition of the customer journey online, has meant that those businesses that focus on customer satisfaction through well thought out customer engagement, have reaped the most rewards. Having the customer journey clearly mapped out, analysed and aligned with digital marketing activity, enables business to eliminate waste and focus on resources and initiatives that have proven to be profitable.

Online sales funnels software constitute a major part in this evolution. An indispensable tool in mapping and managing the buyers' journey, they have come a long way from their traditional marketing inception. Aiding the business owner from acquisition through to conversion and advocacy. All while becoming increasingly accessible, regardless of one's programming knowledge or technical expertise.

Business, particularly SME's, need to stay ahead of the curve when it comes to digital marketing. Familiarize themselves with new practice, while keeping abreast of innovation to remain competitive and grow.

What can be said is that any online business can simply not afford to ignore digital marketing if they want to stay competitive. It will continue to drive innovation on the internet, just as the internet drives innovation in digital marketing.

So, the next time you see a banner ad, take a moment and try to appreciate it. After all, they probably won't be around forever, and the internet simply wouldn't be the way it is today without a little bit of digital marketing.

3.0 INTRODUCING WEB ANALYTICS AND FUNNELS

For any online business, the first step towards achieving success is by creating a meaningful digital footprint. At the very least, a website with sales pages that elegantly articulates products, and generates conversions. Profits aside, how can you measure and track your buyer journey? What sort of penetration does your brand awareness have and exactly where are visitors coming from? How did they hear about your business and how many simply leave without purchasing anything? That is where web analytics and funnels come in. As a business owner, you do not have an infinite capacity of resources, so understanding these answers and how they factor into the growth of your business, means more efficient use of your time, money, and effort.

So, what exactly is web analytics?

> " … is used extensively to track and monitor user interaction patterns with websites by clicking and streaming data or information. This process involves the collection, analysis, as well as reporting of web-based data generated from these interactions, which provide insight into the customer's demand and interest."
>
> – GlobalNewsWire, 2020

Ok, so what does this mean in *English*? It is the process of measuring your business's digital initiatives, analysing the data gathered from it, and using that data to improve your business performance. However, it is not just about quantifying online behaviour but extends to analysing social, campaign, mobile, competitors, survey, and even offline data influenced by the web. Another key purpose is to gain meaningful insights that can help maximize the return on your marketing investment. Without that relevant data and insight, you are essentially flying blind – something that you cannot afford to do as an online business owner.

Web analytical software and statistics are intentionally geared to identifying website visitor patterns and helping you use that knowledge to convert them into customers. This is done through gathering data, such as the number of visits to landing pages that prove to be the most converting. Such data typically takes the form of:

- Web traffic reports
- E-mail response rates
- Direct mail campaign data
- Sales and lead information
- User performance data, for example, click heat mapping
- Bounce rate
- Other custom-made financial and non-financial metrics

CHAPTER 3.0 INTRODUCING WEB ANALYTICS AND FUNNELS

Key Performance Indicators (KPI) are identified and used to measure performance. Data such as those listed above, is compared against KPI's to study visitor response and help improve marketing activity. They remain exclusive to your business and are developed as per your business goals and marketing strategy. All of this data underpins the performance and optimisation of your sales funnel. We will discuss metrics and KPI's in more detail in Chapter 7. So how does this all actually work in practice? Let's go through a brief, yet concise guide to demonstrate.

Figure 3.0.0 – Sample web traffic report

Enter the traffic report, a list of numbers, and information about how visitors are interacting with your site, graphically displaying metrics such as those mentioned above. The backbone of web analytics, this report is used as a means to draw conclusions and adjust your marketing strategy. Moreover, it provides a way to measure your e-commerce sales, goals, and marketing campaign activity. Lastly, it demonstrates keywords that are driving traffic and attribution (the different traffic sources that led to conversions).

Web Analytical tools come in two guises:

1. **Process Log File** – During a website visit, the webserver records some basic information in a file called a *log*. The web analytical tool then crunches through thousands, if not millions, of lines in these log files to create understandable reports. This comes with some drawbacks, namely very large log files to manage and a greater degree of technical expertise to configure.

   Examples: Splunk, Sumo Logic, Logz.io, Graylog, LogDNA, Scalyr, Elastic Cloud, Google Cloud Logging.

   User: Typically requiring larger IT teams to set up, configure, and maintain. Ideally suited to larger organisations with large volumes of web traffic.

2. **JavaScript Based** – The data is received from JavaScript-based web bug reporters. A special snippet of JavaScript is placed on every page of your website. That small piece of code fires whenever someone visits the page, sending data back to the web analytical tool about the visitor. This allows for greater precision and the ability to better measure your campaign performance. However, the main drawback here is the slowing down of page performance, which could impact overall site performance and impede user experience.

   Examples: Google Analytics, Mixpanel, Crazy Egg, Heap, Matomo, StatCounter, Adobe Analytics

   User: SME's, requiring instant and accurate web analytics with close campaign marketing alignment.

As you will come to realise through this book, web analytics are central to your sales funnels. The information they extrapolate has a direct bearing on your sales funnel development, success, and ultimately optimisation. Indeed, most software vendors offering sales funnel products are coupled with web analytical servicing tools. Therein lies the reason why you should have a fundamental understanding of the subject.

Sales funnels are one of the building blocks of digital marketing web analytics. It is based on the premise that prospects and customers go through a step-by-step process – otherwise known as a funnel – before they finally avail themselves of your services and products. A typical sales funnel may look somewhat like this:

CHAPTER 3.0 INTRODUCING WEB ANALYTICS AND FUNNELS 21

Figure 3.0.1 – A typical funnel flow

1. After performing a search for a particular product, a user comes across your online promotional offer.

2. The customer is intrigued and wanting to find out more, clicks on the ad banner.

3. The ad redirects them to your website product landing page.

4. The customer reads the details of the product and offer. Still not quite convinced, they go on to read the customer testimonials.

5. Feeling confident, they decide to purchase and click the "Add-to Cart" button.

6. The quick, simple, and seamless process for checkout further embed their trust and they conclude the transaction.

7. Upon delivery and their satisfaction with the product, they feel compelled to tell others of this offer.

Here is where web analytics and funnels come into play. Not everyone who saw the ad clicked on it, and not everyone who clicked, went on to add the product to the cart. Furthermore, some visitors added the product to the cart but then changed their mind at the last minute, ending the transaction by failing to check out. In this instance, web analytics can provide metrics such as ad views, ad clicks, product, and checkout page visits. As for the funnel, those would be the steps you identify in this journey that lead to conversion, something akin to:

1. Clicked ad
2. Viewed product
3. Added to cart
4. Checked out
5. Paid
6. Order confirmed

Web analytics, combined with your funnel, will help you understand how many people dropped out at what stage in the journey, leading to a better understanding of your customer behaviour. You can then use this knowledge to optimise the sales process, translating that into sales and helping you move toward achieving your business goals.

3.1 A QUICK FUNNEL SETUP

Google Analytics is arguably the most common and accessible tool for performing web analytics. Being freely available, it is apt for the website manager novice. It provides a variety of tools that track and report website traffic, as a platform inside the Google Marketing Platform brand. Key amongst these tools is an online sales funnels feature, which provides you the means to easily set up and track your customer's behaviour as they step through your sales process. Hence, we are using this as an example; however, there are notably many other software products available and these are discussed in depth in Chapter 8.

Google Analytics uses the concept of *Goals* to help you measure how often visitors on your website complete specific actions, and how your website fulfils your target objectives. A website goal is a finished activity (referred to as a conversion) that contributes towards the success of your business. For example, in e-commerce, your website goal could be customers checking out after making a purchase. It could be getting customers to sign up for your newsletter, or getting 500 people to download your pdf.

Whatever your goal is, remember that there is a funnel your customers have to go through before they reach that goal. Setting up that funnel will highlight the customers' journey through each step that you define, subsequently enabling you to see where they dropped off during the journey and providing you the opportunity to rectify whatever issues resulted in the drop-off.

> **"** A website goal is a finished activity (referred to as a conversion) that contributes towards the success of your business.

There are different types of goals in Google Analytics:

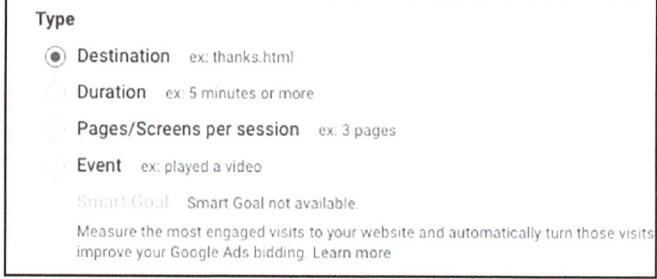

Figure 3.1.1 – Goal types

Destination Goals: This is when a user is viewing a designated page or screen. In terms of conversion, it is mostly a page – like a thank you page – that is displayed after someone fills out a form or orders something from your site.

Duration Goals: These track how long someone spends on a particular page in your site, or how much time they spend on the site altogether.

Pages/Screens per Session: This looks at how many pages a user visits on your webpage before they sign out or close the website.

Event Goals: This tracks when a user performs a specified action, like watching a video or playing a game.

A goal funnel is perfect for beginners who want detailed, correct, and precise information that they can further expand to make more comprehensive reports. To use a goal funnel in Google Analytics, you need to set up a Goal and state the funnel path.

Case Study:

Winter Parka – A winter clothing outlet, based out in suburban Anchorage, Alaska. Sells all manner of winter coats and parkas, with an e-commerce (albeit fictitious) sales website: www.WinterParka.inc. Your end game is to generate leads to buy your products from your online store.

The first thing you need to do is set up a goal:

1. Log in to Google Analytics, select a profile and click on **Admin** in the side menu.

2. Select **Goals** from the View column, then click on **New Goal** [Continue].

3. Select the **Custom** option from Goal Setup.

4. Enter a Goal name (e.g. Coats Purchase).

5. Select the Goal **Type** Destination [Continue].

6. In Goal Details, leave the Destination as **Equals to.**

7. Enter a Goal URL, such as /thank-you.php.

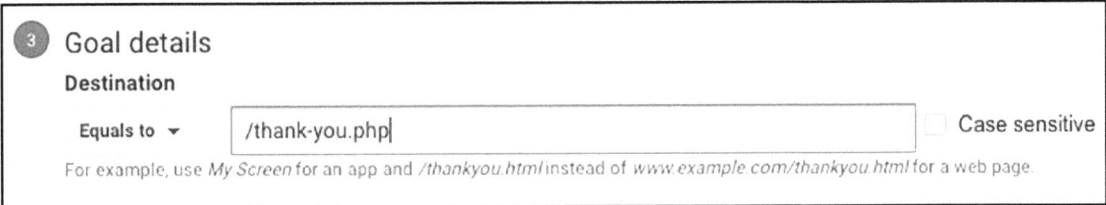

Figure 3.1.2 – Goal details

Before you save your goal, you can choose to set up your funnel.

To set up your funnel:

8. Turn on the "Funnel" Switch.

9. Name each step of the funnel and add a URL to each. For example;

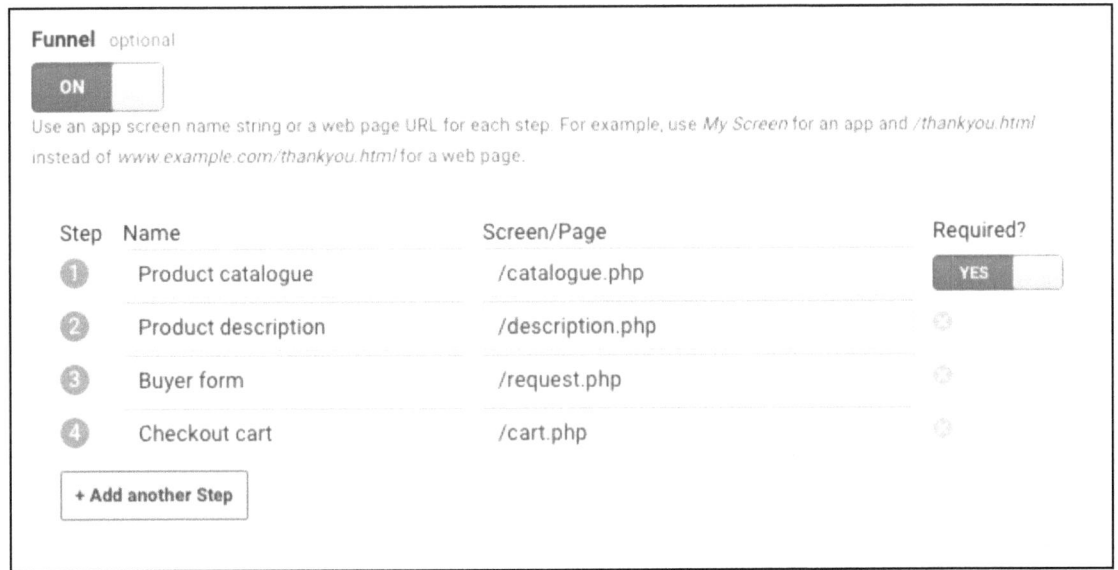

Figure 3.1.3 – Funnel steps

24 CHAPTER 3.0 INTRODUCING WEB ANALYTICS AND FUNNELS

10. Select the **Required Step** checkbox for the first funnel step.
11. Step 10 is often recommended for generating simpler funnel data but is not obligatory.
12. All done.

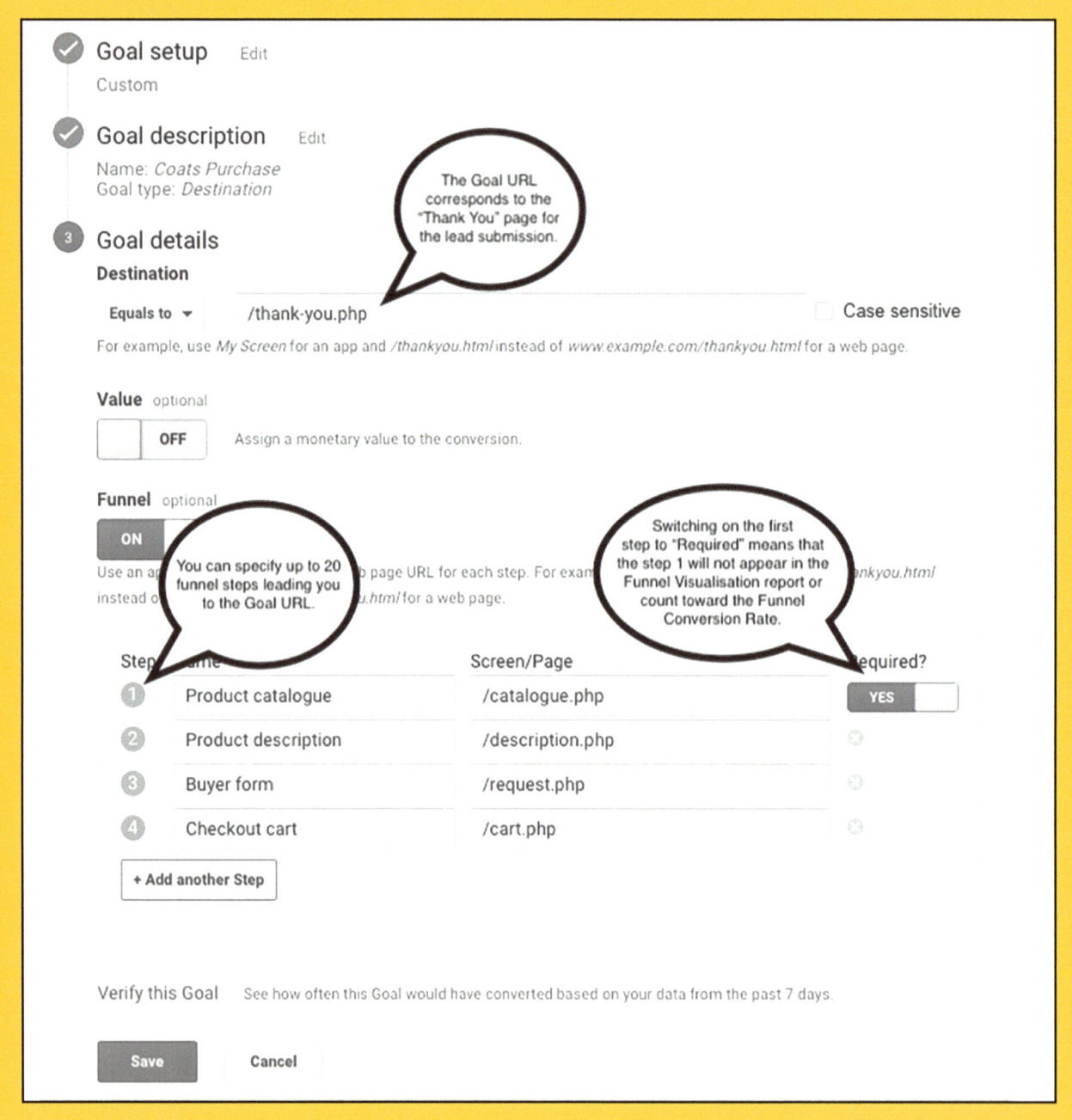

Figure 3.1.4 – Google Analytics Funnel setup

Let's assume that thank-you.php appears after the successful online payment for a product. You now have the means to see how many customers are successfully purchasing after having first viewed your products, through filling out an account form and clearing the checkout process. More importantly, if they fail to transact, you can now see exactly during which stage in the journey they are dropping off. This is a rather simplistic example, but it demonstrates the core principles behind the sales funnel theory.

Once all the required configuration is entered, the results will be visible under "Conversions" on your Google Analytics website. Under the "Goals" section, you will be able to access many reports that will help you learn about your user and customer behaviour.

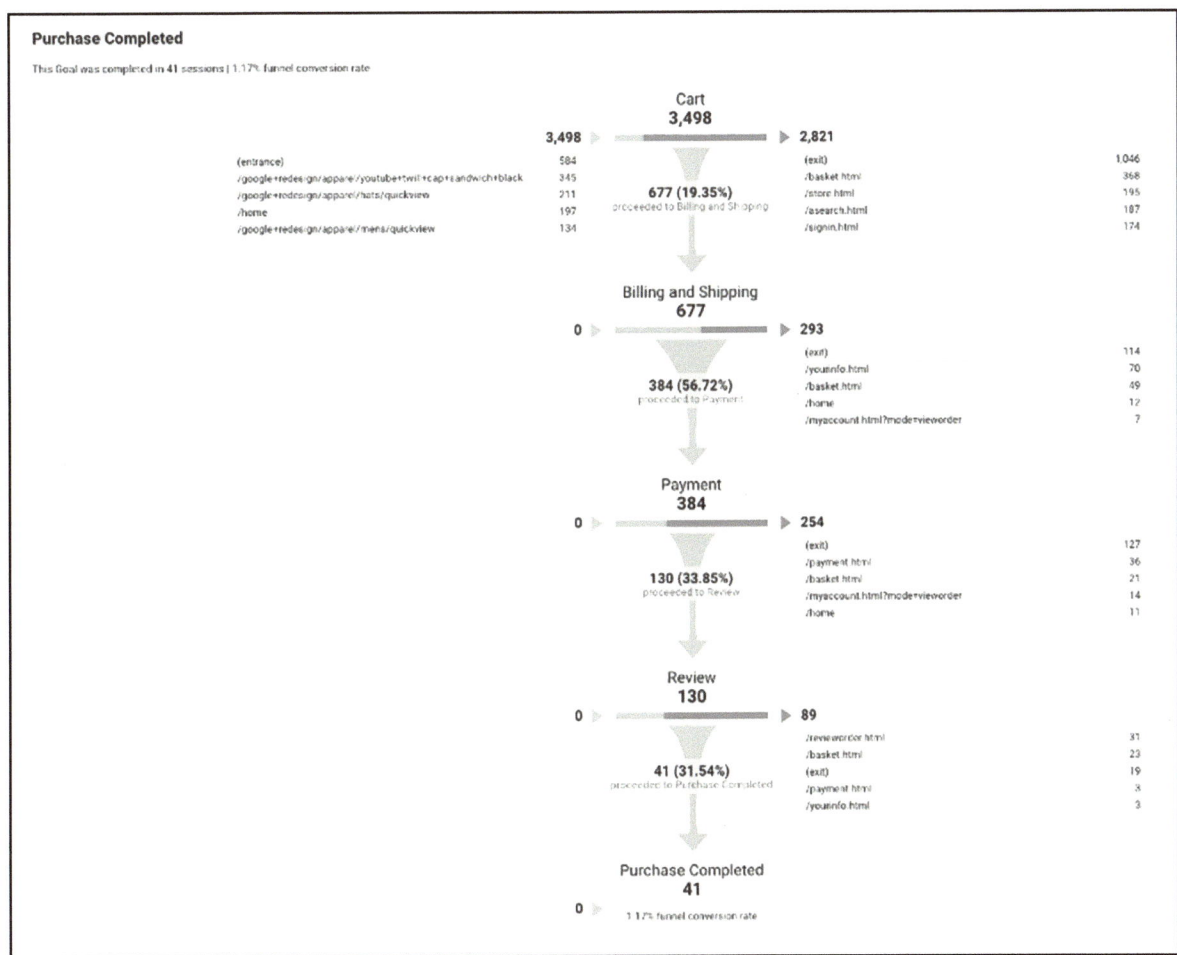

Figure 3.1.5 – Sample Google Analytics Funnel report

Such a report shows you exactly how many visitors are stepping through the process and will help you highlight the following:

- Biggest Abandonment points: In the sample, you will see that only 19% of over 3,000 visitors that had items in the Cart, proceeded to Billing and Shipping. This is substantial, so focusing on what is the cause will increase the overall conversion rate.

- Unexpected Entry Points: Visitors may not necessarily follow the flow. For example, they may be on the Cart page and then decided to browse around a little more. They then entered the Billing and Shipping page from an altogether different page, which could mean that you should add a more obvious "Checkout" CTA.

The idea here is to give you a quick and simple introduction to what online sales funnels are and how easy they are to set up. It is, therefore, deliberately brief with its Google Analytics detail. For more comprehensive tutorials on Google Analytics and Funnel setup, visit:
https://analytics.google.com/analytics/web

4.0 MAPPING THE BUYER'S JOURNEY

A customer journey is a story about understanding your users, how they behave while they visit your website, and what you can do to improve their trip so that they keep coming back.

In marketing terms, there are three distinct levels to the buyer's journey:

1. Awareness: The buyer realises that they have a problem or a need, but they are not entirely sure what it is yet. At this stage, more clarification is required to understand that specific need or problem. To address the buyer, the marketer creates content that directly addresses their problem. The buyer is not quite ready to buy anything yet, they just want their problems addressed and articulated in a way that they can relate to. Low-pressure content like videos, blogs, and guides will help the buyer understand their problem and outline their next line of action.

2. Consideration: At this stage, the buyer finally understands what their problem is and now begins to research various solutions. Here, your duty as a digital marketer is to position your product or services in a way that makes the buyer give proper consideration to you. How? By creating in-depth and thoughtful content that recognizes different approaches to solving the buyer's problems, i.e., encouraging the buyer to request product demonstrations, start free trials, download e-books, or register for a newsletter. This stage is a great point to recognise possible good leads. After all, if they sign-up to download your e-book, it means they are interested in what you have to offer.

3. Decision Stage: Here, the buyer has several services and products that they are interested in, and may even possibly have created a list of potential suppliers to fulfil them. They are actively seeking a vendor that best suits their needs. So far, you have addressed the buyer's problems and proffered possible solutions. This is where you go in for the catch and the conversion. Create persuasive content that tells the buyer that yours is the best solution. Openly promote your services and products. Express the advantages of your methods and provide success stories and case studies that your methods have helped. Be honest, inspire confidence, and back up your claims with verifiable data. Content that you can use here includes instructional tutorials, videos, success stories, and your product documentation.

Over the years, various tools and techniques have evolved online to capture the buyer's attention, for each stage through this journey. Here we discuss a mere sample that stands out to us as being exceptionally practical and effective:

Create Lead Magnets: These are incentives that marketers offer to potential buyers in exchange for their email address or other contact information. Such tools help you gather valuable information from your prospects by enabling the creation of lead magnets such as white papers, quizzes, webinars, and eBooks. You should begin to use these regularly, as you churn out such digital content periodically, aligned with marketing campaign activity:

Designrr.io
A tool to help you to automate the process of transforming your blog posts, videos, and podcasts into flipbooks, eBooks, and transcripts that you can use as lead magnets.

Canva.com
Is a simple design tool that helps you render your images, infographics, and promotional materials in a few short steps.

Typeform.com
Helps you create interactive experiences with your audience. With lots of templates to choose from, creating quizzes and surveys, and analysing them is made easy.

Wishpond.com
Enables you to create landing pages and social media contests, send emails, and track your leads.

Create Converting Landing Pages: In digital marketing, a landing page is a standalone web page, created specifically for marketing campaign activity. It's where a visitor "lands" after being redirected from a place on the web such as a link in an email, or ads from Google. When designed properly, the landing page is a tool that can both collect leads and close sales. A good landing page gives you more space to work with and removes unnecessary distractions so that visitors to your website can focus on your selling points. Fortunately, there are several ideal tools that can help you build a great landing page amongst them are:

Leadpages.com Is a powerful landing page builder that helps create high-converting landing pages and drive sales for businesses. It has lead generation and opt-in tools integrated.

Landingi.com
Is a user-friendly platform to create, launch, and optimize landing pages, pop-ups, and funnels to boost the results of your marketing efforts.

Visualise Your Funnels: These tools help you build complex funnels in a digital format and present an accurate visual representation to aid your customer journey mapping. Such tools provide clarity of the whole process and how sales funnels can be better optimized.

FunnelFlows.com
Is a tool for rapidly crafting professional marketing funnel flowcharts perfectly. It makes complicated funnel flows easy.

Funnelytics.io
Is an all-in-one mapping and tracking tool for your sales funnel.

Utilise Lead Generation Tools: These are tools that help in initiating consumer interest or inquiry into your business, products, or services. Engagement is paramount to developing qualified leads, so tools that can initiate this and help in identify leads to follow-up, are particularly useful:

Intercom.com Is a tool that helps you build better customer relationships through conversational, messenger-based experiences.

Snitcher.com Is software that integrates with your Google Analytics profile to retroactively identify who has visited your site, how they found you, and what they were looking for.

Build Email Automation: An important aspect of email marketing is the capability to send time or action triggered emails to subscribers with relevant information. By mechanizing your whole lead nurturing process, also allows you to build relationships with clients through on-going communication, sending them relevant, valid, and useful content:

SendinBlue.com Is a powerful email automation software that enables you to send the right message at the right time.

ActiveCampaign.com Allows you to send personalized emails, create triggers for emails based on events like email opens and link clicks, organize your sales information, and set-up your whole nurturing sequence.

At each stage of your buyer's journey, there is a tool available to help. The key thing is to do your research and compare in terms of fit, cost, and benefit. Each also comes with a varying degree of learning required, so make sure you choose ones that you're completely comfortable with on a technical level.

5.0 SALES FUNNELS: A COMPREHENSIVE GUIDE

Quintessentially, the sales funnel is an outline of the steps taken by a visitor in becoming a customer. Furthermore, it is a detailed depiction of those steps to not just becoming customers, but also becoming your advocates and ultimately your publicists.

The sales funnel differs from the buyer's journey in that the sales funnel is from your business's perspective and the buyer's journey is from the buyer's point of view. The buyer is not concerned with whether or not your business can turn leads into conversions or gain new customers. As long as the buyer can move through awareness, consideration, and decision stages as soon as possible, the buyer is satisfied. You? Not so much, if the buyer fails to perform that all-important purchase action.

This chapter aims to make you understand the funnel's importance and how harnessing it correctly can do wonders for the growth of your business. You will learn why you need to be aware of it conceptually, the benefits of an effective funnel, and the different types and models available. We will also touch upon how to turn leads into conversions, cost implications, and the distinction between marketing and sales versions.

5.1 BACKGROUND

The concept was developed in 1898 by Elias St. Elmo Lewis, an advertising agency executive. He theorized outlining the buyer's journey and breaking it down into four stages: Awareness, Interest, Desire, and Action – AIDA.

Awareness – The customer is aware of the existence of a product or service.

Interest – Actively express an interest in a product group.

Desire – Aspires to a particular brand or product.

Action – Actively taking the next step towards purchasing a chosen product.

Although there are variations to Lewis' funnels, the basics remain the same, and most sales funnels today are derivatives of this initial thought process. In the modern digital era, several sales funnel models have become apparent, leading to wide acceptance that additional stages are warranted to the basic AIDA model. This is due in part to technological innovation and a need to accommodate evolving customer behaviour. Regardless, the sales funnel remains the cornerstone of marketing campaigns, probing the customer journey, and lead management.

5.2 WINTER PARKA – A SALES FUNNEL STORY

The funnel is more than just a visual representation of the buyer's journey from first contact, to completing a purchase. To fathom the different stages of the sales funnel, let's consider that fictional company again from chapter 3.0 – Winter Parka, the uber-cool retail store selling coats and parkas in Alaska.

Winter Parka launches an advertising campaign for people who require warm, comfortable outdoor coats and parkas for extreme conditions. They run an online marketing campaign, offering a 30% discount coupon code in exchange for subscribing to their email list. Over time, this activity is getting them noticed.

CHAPTER 5.0 SALES FUNNELS: A COMPREHENSIVE GUIDE

Figure 5.2.1 – The linear funnel model

4,000 (*visitors* at this stage) view the ads. 1,000 click, directing them to the Winter Parka promotional landing page. This stage is **Awareness**, and those 1,000 people just turned from visitors into *prospects*.

The next stage of the funnel is **Interest**. Of the 1,000 prospects, only 500 people are actually interested in coats and parkas. Why should they buy from Winter Parka? What is their return and refund policy? Are there other businesses that are closer by, selling similar products with more competitive pricing? The prospects research, compare and mull over their options. At the end of this stage, only 300 people become interested enough to consider purchasing from them. After all, a business based in a place as cold as Alaska must know their stuff when comes to winter clothing, right?

The third stage of the funnel is **Desire**. The prospects delve more into Winter Parka's website and decide to subscribe to their email list in return for the coupon code. 200 people fill out the forms, and just became *leads*. At this point, Winter Parka can reach them outside of their website by sending them follow-up emails.

The 200 leads receive emails from Winter Parka. 50 leads decide they do not need a coat or parka after all; the ones they bought from last winter still do the trick. 10 leads found another business where they have similar products at lower prices, albeit inferior quality. 5 leads do not remember signing up for coupons and wonder why Winter Parka sent them an email? 15 leads just couldn't be bothered to open the email. However, 120 finally take action. They order from Winter Parka and complete the fourth stage of **Action** to become *buyers*.

At the end of the fourth stage of the funnel, Winter Parka had gained just 120 from an initial 1,000 prospects. However 18 buyers did not like the size of their Parka, and 2 ordered beige in Cosmic Latte but got Tuscan instead. So, they definitely will not be buying from Winter Parka again. The remaining 100 loved their purchase and will most likely buy from Winter Parka again; they have completed the fifth stage of **Loyalty** to become true *customers*.

The sixth and final stage of this sales funnel is **Advocacy**. 15 customers are satisfied with their purchase, and to them, that is the end of it. 85 customers loved Winter Parka so much that they just cannot stop talking about their experience and products to friends and family, encouraging them to buy from Winter Parka too. They have gone beyond being loyal customers to become *brand advocates*.

From the start, it is apparent why the sales funnel is widest at the top and narrowest at its bottom. Many more people are active in the earliest stages of the funnel than they are at the latter ones. At each stage of the funnel, more qualified prospects are pushed towards the next stage, and less qualified prospects are dropped out of the funnel.

Note: Sales funnels are not always as clear cut as this; you can have unexpected entry points. Prospects could have quite easily purchased straight after completing the offer form, without receiving the follow-up email or decided to visit the store upon seeing the ad. The idea here is to embed the principles behind the stages by demonstrating a clean journey.

5.3 JOURNEY BY METHOD

Awareness: At this stage, you need to cast a very wide net for your prospects. A presence across all marketing boards and channels will help you accomplish this. People with a problem need to become aware that your company, products, or services are the answer. We list a few proven methods below to help you.

a. *Google*:
   When most people have a question that needs an immediate answer, the de facto response is to go online and Google it. People resort to Google to answer the most basic questions that they have. Your prospects and customers are the same. Google has about 3.5 billion searches every day and 90% of the search engine market share. So it stands to reason that this is where you need to rank well. People need to be able to find your content, read it, and think of you as someone who can address their problem. Ensure you have relevant, pertinent content that is full of buzz words, derived from thorough keyword research. Use Search Engine Optimisation (SEO) to ensure that every one of your posts has search traffic potential. See links below for help with getting you started:

https://ads.google.com/intl/en_uk/home/tools/keyword-planner/ – Google keyword tool.

https://search.google.com/search-console/about – Google search console (SEO) tool.

https://www.semrush.com/ – Popular paid software tool for keyword and SEO services.

b. *YouTube*:
   With one billion users, YouTube is the second-largest search engine in the world. However, it is still pretty much neglected for business purposes. It is more than likely that you will find a large pool of your customers here.

The process is similar to that of Google. Use keyword research to find out what people are watching on YouTube and use that to inform your decisions on what to post. Create high quality, actionable videos that rank well:

https://studio.youtube.com/ – Manage presence, grow, and interact with your audience.

https://www.youtube.com/creators/ – Official home for creator resources and benefits.

c. ***Online Communities***: Places like Quora, Reddit, Facebook Groups, and Slack Communities may not rank as high as Google on the search engine lists, but they provide a personalized, nuanced experience that Google cannot. Online communities are places where people with common interests gather, and the traffic that these online communities garner may be just what you need to grow your customer pool. The process is simple: regularly share tips and participate in discussions. However, read and follow the rules of every community. Disobeying the rules will result in you getting ejected. Add value to the community. Do not spam. Once you are a trusted member, you can then start to promote your brand:

https://organizedassistant.com/use-reddit-promote-business/ – Simple and creative tips for business promotion on Reddit.

https://www.postplanner.com/use-facebook-groups-for-marketing-business/ – 6 Clever Ways to Use Facebook Groups for Marketing Your Business.

https://www.socialmediaexaminer.com/26-ways-to-market-your-business-with-tumblr/ – 26 Ways to Market Your Business with Tumblr.

d. ***Influencers:*** Influencers have an audience across several social platforms. Use them to expose your brand and message to an entirely new group of people. Build a list of influencers that you would like to work with. Next, send them personalized emails to see if they would love to work with you. Let them understand what is in it for them and what you are willing to offer them:

https://www.singlegrain.com/content-marketing-strategy-2/guide-influencer-marketing/ – Guide to Growing Your Business with Influencer Marketing.

Interest: At this stage, you have managed to hook your potential customers. They have consumed your content; they now need to know more. You need to start ranking well for specific search queries, so when performed by prospects, they will find you. For example, instead of searching for "winter coats and parka", they may begin looking for SEO-specific terms like "fur-lined parka" or "100% wool coats." You need to be the expert that your prospects need you to be. Gently nudge them into the next stage by demonstrating how your product or service can solve their problem.

a. Rank for topics with high business potential: This is based on the premise that your customers are now making those more specific searches. Perform keyword research into these granular terms. These are not just relevant to your business, but also address problems that your products or services solve. The goal is to rank highly for them. Teach them how to solve that problem, and how your problem or service can help. Let's consider Winter Parka again. The company became aware of a common issue whereby coats are prone to piling, losing their integrity, and therefore not durable over the years. To tap into this problem, they create blog content that advocates nylon blends, supporting their track record of being strong and lasting. In the process addressing a customer concern, ranking in such queries, and ultimately steering prospects to their products.

b. *Get them to follow you:* Now that they think your content is valuable, they are your fans. Whilst this is positive, what you want is for them to be customers. Maybe there was an issue that led to them not to take that final purchasing action. Find out what they need by using your social media platforms like Facebook, YouTube, and Twitter. Put up call-to-actions that remind them to subscribe, like, follow or sign up to your email list. Ideally, you need to offer them multiple touchpoints for them to follow you. For example, newsletter or YouTube subscription or joining your Facebook group. All of which amounts to an opportunity for you to move them along the funnel and perform that all-important purchase.

Desire: At this stage, your prospects know that they have a problem, they know the solution to the problem, and that you can help. The only issue is, you are not the only one capable of this fulfilment. There are alternatives out there. Your job is to make sure they choose you; but how do we go about doing this?

a. Promote aspects of your unique value points. For example, at Winter Parka, they are particularly proud of their ethical environmental support and involvement. A percentage of all sales are given to Alaskan wildlife preservation trusts. Together with this and content demonstrating their work in preservation is the key to their brand.

b. Attempt to be reviewed on third-party websites where prospects can independently gauge your products, services, and brand. Be this in the form of customers or consumer choice companies, getting favourable ratings and feedback is key. This goes a long way than simply having recommendations on your website.

c. Another common factor in prospect consideration is product comparison. For example, in the Winter Parka case, prospects may typically perform a search for "winter puffer jacket vs anoraks" or "Best winter coats 2020." Then, they will go on to read the reviews and recommendations. The goal here is for you to dominate those search engine result pages (SERPs). Targeting search queries that include modifier terms such as "vs", "best" and "top."

d. Narrative – Another way to gently ebb those followers is through a sequence that aims to nurture the prospect into a sale. There are various ways to do this, but the most common in the digital space is email-based, by sending out communication that explains why you are different, why buy from you, and preparing them to buy. Essentially an overarching story is what you are trying to communicate here. For example:

- New idea or concept: "Only certain types of winter coat are suitable for temperatures below –10 degrees."

- Teach: "How to look after that expensive parka so that it lasts many winters."

- Announcement: "New line of puffer jackets arriving this autumn."

- Value: "Our parkas are lined with 100% wool, proven to be the most effective material to keep warm."

- Larger story: "How we went from working in the city to selling coats in the wilderness."

These are a selection of examples following an email sequence; there are plenty of other methods to create that narrative – phone calls, blog content, webinars, and video content, to name a few.

Action: At this stage, your prospects are pretty much convinced that you are the answer to their need or problem. What is required here is to provide that final "nudge", make the transaction as comfortable as possible, and maybe use the opportunity for some upsell. As for that "nudge", let's consider some methods:

a) Test before you buy: Free trial periods are an ideal lure, providing a risk-averse option.

b) Utilize urgency: "only 5 left in stock", "end of season clear-out." Please be ethical here and only post genuine content.

c) User experience: We cannot stress enough how critical having a smooth and easy checkout experience is to ensuring purchase, good feedback, and a strong likelihood of a customer returning.

This is also a stage where you attempt some upselling, which is essentially selling add-ons to the product. Examples of add-ons might be phone insurance when purchasing a mobile phone or having the option to "go large" on a fast food meal. However, it would be wise to practice caution here. There are plenty of examples of unethical upselling, where a customer has purchased an add-on unknowingly, and that is a sure-fire way to bad feedback and reputational loss.

SALES FUNNEL AND TIME

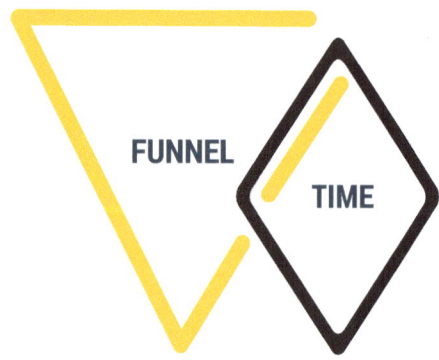

Figure 5.3.1 – Funnel and time inverse relationship

As we saw in the Winter Parka case study, during the early stages of the funnel, people initially have little time for you. Your business is competing with hundreds, possibly thousands of others vying for buyer attention. However, as they begin to note things that resonate, they will dedicate more time to digging deeper. When they have evaluated you and begin to trust you, they will be devoting less and less time to your site.

You need to understand how time affects your marketing strategies. While it may seem a good idea to inundate prospects with information about you once they show interest, it is not actually what your prospects want.

Rather than bombard them with too much information that proves to be overwhelming and unhelpful, it is better to send information that is pertinent, concise, and appropriate. At Winter Parka, if the email sent to each prospect was a 50 product catalogue of clothing, this would not effectively piqued interest as effectively as promoting a handful of best-selling products.

MARKETING FUNNEL: TIME, EMOTION, AND LOGIC

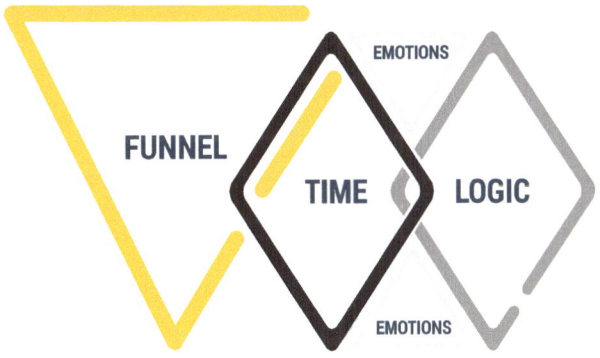

Figure 5.3.2 – Funnel, time, emotion and logic relationship

We now know how time interacts with the funnel, so let us now factor in the dimensions of emotion and logic.

The power of emotions and stories are long-established, from both a psychological point of view and in marketing. Elmer Wheeler's famous technique "Don't sell the steak – sell the sizzle!"

> **Your business is competing with hundreds, possibly thousands of others vying for buyer attention.**

(The New Yorker, 1938), is known colloquially as 'Sales 101', while Tony Robbins tells us that "people don't buy products, they buy feelings."

Both emotion and logic are inversely related as a prospect moves through the sales funnel and directly relates to your message. When you use a visitor's emotion to drive attention, you need to use logic to make them keep that attention fixed on you. Using logic implies letting them understand that you are good at what you do and that you can address whatever they need. When that is accomplished, you need to go back and use emotion to make them buy and gently push them across the line, once they have reached the penultimate stage of your sales funnel.

Let's consider Donald, a Winter Parka prospect, lured through digital marketing. He is smitten by a particularly fetching parka. The product landing page description entices him further with words such as tough, warm, and 'as endorsed by Eskimos' (ok, maybe not the latter, but you get the idea). However, he has concerns surrounding an online purchase from a company he has never dealt with before. So, he uses a third party consumer site, Trustpilot, and reads the numerous reviews and ratings on Winter Parka. Feeling a little more confident, he then explores Winter Parkas' return and refund policy. Now feeling somewhat at ease with his intended purchase, he explores the variety of colours and sizes available. Feeling confident with product quality, the company, the return policy, and product variety – he commits to buying.

5.4 BENEFITS OF THE SALES FUNNEL

> **4,000 people who saw the advertising campaign, and even though 120 people purchased from Winter Parka, only 85 went through all the stages of the sales funnel – that is only less than 3%.**

For anyone looking up from the bottom of Winter Parka sales funnel, 85 brand advocates is an impressive number. With 85 people dedicated to promoting their wares, Winter Parka is potentially looking at a significant amount of new sales, all without any real effort on their part. A person looking down from the top of the sales funnel would have a different opinion. They see 4,000 people who saw the advertising campaign, and even though 120 people purchased from Winter Parka, only 85 went through all the stages of the sales funnel – that is only less than 3%.

This initial analysis demonstrates that something is not quite right either with their customer acquisition, marketing, or sales process. This is where the sales funnel can come to their aid. By having the ability to determine exactly how many people dropped out at each step in the funnel, they can highlight weak spots and bottlenecks, allowing them to focus, directly addressing those areas, and rethinking their content, message, or functionality.

For example, only 1,000 people clicked on the ad when 4,000 saw it. Could there be something wrong with the presentation? Maybe the copy was not quite catchy or interesting enough. Without the sales funnel to give Winter Parka those numbers, they would probably roll out the same ad campaign again and achieve similar results.

Let's say the company came to the realisation that content marketing on the landing page is the issue. Through funnel web analytics, they identified specific page sections to concentrate on, leading them to test more creative copy and imagery, aimed at addressing those excessive drop-off points. With targeted purposeful content, the company became more confident of their marketing strategy and saw a measurably better return in addressing the prospect's problems and needs.

Their next several marketing campaigns included further revisions to address weak spots. Which saved them time, money, and resources through more efficient campaign activity. By repeating the same process of analysis, test, and revision, they were able to fine-tune their marketing activity by noting what worked well and what did not. By experimenting further, they landed on proven ways that ensured a better return on conversions.

There is a reason why the funnel is widest at the top – to catch a large group that then filters down to customers. However, following funnel analysis, 'catch-all' becomes increasingly full of more likely prospects and customers. You may find fewer people entering the top, but you will find greater numbers leaving the bottom. For example, Winter Parka begin to target their ads to people that actively search for specific coats and parkas, not just generic winter clothing. As your changes become more focused and your experimentation yields more results, you will find increasing confidence in your campaigns.

Key points:

> - Helps determine at what stage people leave the buyer journey, how many, and why.
>
> - Highlights steps in the sales process where focus is required.
>
> - Drives more targeted, pertinent marketing campaigns.
>
> - Improves sales through more efficient marketing activity.

5.5 FUNNEL ANALYSIS

There is method in measuring how visitors interact and navigate through your buyer's journey. Enabling you to track drop off, conversion rate, and campaign success.

- Funnel analysis gives you a much clearer picture of where, how, and why visitors to your website are dropping off.

- Discovering new opportunities for growth and how those opportunities can be optimized.

- Identifying the performance of your advertising campaigns, and helping you prepare a more efficient marketing strategy.

- Visualising website visitors into paying customers, by walking them through your sales funnel.

Improving your conversion rate and provide visibility on what is working, what is not, and where changes need to be made.

Steps Involved in Funnel Analysis

- Monitor important business Key Performance Indicators (KPIs). Every stage of the funnel contains important information and metrics working together to present a complete picture. Some key ones:

    i   Total number of conversions of the entire funnel during a specific reporting period.

    ii Number of daily sign-ups and active users for platform conversion funnels.

    iii Customer and revenue churn rates – the rate at which customers are dropping off and the subsequent impact on revenue.

- Build multiple funnels and track them all for optimal conversion.

- Utilise heatmaps to help you understand user behaviour. Heatmaps are graphical representations of data, where a matrix represents values as colours. In this case, it demonstrates where the most activity occurs on the website.

- Visualise your funnel: This will help you get a clear picture of your funnel for analysis. Enabling you to take measurable action for optimisation.

- Reorder your funnel – This is a way to test the funnel for flexibility and to investigate all possibilities for improvement in the customer journey.

How to Get Actionable Insights from Your Funnel

There are three major ways to do this:
1. Bottleneck Check: The goal here is to check areas where people are dropping off the most in the funnel. If the number of people checking out on an e-commerce website is only a negligible fraction of those that clicked the landing page, there may be a bottleneck, such as a complicated process, or a difficult-to-navigate website.
2. Time Delay Check: This is the time that a website visitor takes to get from one stage of the funnel to the other. Analysing the reasons why there are delays between two consecutive stages of the funnel can reveal a lot about the quality of your products and services, and your communication methods with your customers.
3. User Segmentation: Keeping your users segmented based on demography or behaviour will help you understand why some user-segments are more successful at certain steps than others. It will also help you answer some cogent questions such as what kind of users you need to target in the future, why other user categories get stuck in the funnel, and why certain user categories churn the most.

Strengths and Limitations of Funnel Analysis

Strengths:
- Helps you highlight the most important areas in the user journey that are the primary causes of dropout.
- Can identify specific areas where content is not up-to-par or inversely, where content is proving to be the most successful for conversion.

Limitations:
- Determining what users to include and ones to exclude from the funnel is not easy.
- It is not ideal to use a single funnel to measure performance in platform-oriented websites where multiple workflows can exist simultaneously.
- Customers tend to jump funnel stages or move back and forth between stages, making it difficult to pinpoint the number of conversions and drop-offs at each stage successfully.

Best Practices for Funnel Analysis

- Capture the movement of your funnel by taking pictures at regular intervals.
- Analyse every change in field history values that your capturing reveals.
- Check for every pitfall that has the potential to kill your conversion rates.
- Make small improvements at every conversion step so that you can fully understand the impact that every change has on the overall funnel.
- Measure your funnel velocity (rate of change of a prospect into a lead or a customer). This gives you an account of how quickly or slowly prospects move through your funnel. You should also look at the velocity of each stage of the funnel to pinpoint the bottlenecks and time delays.
- Once you have an idea of funnel velocity, movement, and conversion rates, it will give you a better idea of the future of your funnel. This will in turn help you to make better and more accurate forecasts that will impact your business and inform you of the next steps.

How to Optimize Your Funnel

- Set up your funnel goals and define them.
- Use proper headlines on your landing pages. Find the ones that have the most impact on engagement and conversion and use them.
- Provide useful information in your content. Study your website visitors' behaviour and learn what they interact with the most.
- Use colours and backgrounds that explore the proper equilibrium between your brand identity and your website's page conversion rates.
- Use various fonts and font sizes to give an aesthetically pleasing result.
- Use pages and graphics that load faster. Visitors do not have the time or patience to wait around if your pages load at a slow speed.
- Test the usability of your website by receiving feedback from users in real-time.

5.6 B2B AND B2C FUNNELS

Broadly speaking, there are two types of sales and consequently, sales funnels – Business-to-Business (B2B) and Business-to-Consumer (B2C).
Marketers aim to capture the attention of these two distinct audiences, and although there are many similarities between these types of marketing, how they engage audiences on each channel is quite different.

The B2C sales funnel aims to sell products to individuals harbouring an intent to make a personal purchase. In most cases, the buyer need not obtain permission from anyone in performing the transaction. The sole responsibility and decision-making power rests with the buyer. The B2B buyer on the other hand is often a group of people, in which there are various influencers and multiple decision-makers. On an average, about five people sign off on a B2B transaction. As a result, the B2B sales funnel takes considerably longer to step through than its B2C counterpart.

Another distinction between the two is motivation. Individual buyers are often driven by emotion and personal motives. B2B buyers are far more logical and consider every aspect of the product or service before proceeding with the purchase. A lot hangs in the balance on their purchasing and business decisions, so they cannot afford to be irrational.

Customer relationships also differ widely between the two. B2C buyers rarely speak to a customer care representative before making their purchase. Whereas in B2B, several sales and customer care representatives are guiding and helping through all the stages of the funnel until they are ready to finalize their deal.

The best platforms to implement a B2B sales funnel are professional networks that create connections between specialists and business executives. One such network is LinkedIn, which has well over 630 million members and over 260 million monthly active users. A B2B marketer can use such a platform to network with influencers from all over the world. More personal social media platforms like Facebook, Twitter, and Instagram are better suited to B2C marketing.

CHAPTER 5.0 SALES FUNNELS: A COMPREHENSIVE GUIDE

Search Engine Marketing (SEM) and paid ads on platforms such as LinkedIn and Google are some of the more fruitful strategies in B2B marketing. However, businesses are unlikely to search for products and services on social media. The opposite can be said for B2C marketing. Connecting on a personal note with an audience, engaging with them, and creating brand awareness here goes a long way to help you drive traffic.

As a business owner, being aware of the difference between the B2B and B2C sales funnels, should help you direct your marketing strategy and campaigns, and enable you to broadcast the right communication to the right audience, with the most effective content.

5.7 COSTS & CONVERSIONS

An essential term in sales funnels theory to be aware of is 'conversion rate', which is defined as:

> **"The percentage of visitors to your website that complete a desired goal (a conversion) out of the total number of visitors."**
>
> – Wordstream.com

An e-commerce site that receives 200 visitors in a month and has 50 sales, the conversion rate would be 50 divided by 200, or 25%. Costs refer to conversion expenditure, for example, how much it cost to convert a visitor into a prospect.

In the sales funnel context, there are two kinds of conversion rates that you should be aware of:

1. In-process conversion rate
2. Overall conversion rate

In-process conversions deal with the various stages of the sales funnel. For simplicity, let's consider the standard AIDA model:

- 1st Awareness stage (CA)
- 2nd Interest stage (CI)
- 3rd Desire stage (CD)
- 4th Action stage (CAc)

With the four in-process conversion rates, the overall conversion rate (C) can be calculated using this formula

 C = (CA x CI x CD x CAc)

In the Winter Parka case study, recall that the advertisement was seen by 4,000 people. They represent the Entrance to the funnel:

- **1,000 people** clicked on the advertisement to become aware of Winter Parka's business. That represents 25% of the Entrance.

- **500 people** considered buying from Winter Parka, representing 50% of the Awareness stage.

- **200 people** had the desire to buy, representing 40% of the Interest stage.

- **Only 120 people** finally purchased products from Winter Parka, representing 60% of the Desire stage.

Entrance	Awareness	Interest	Desire	Action
4000	1000	500	200	120
	CA = 25%	CI = 50%	CD = 40%	CP = 60%

Table 5.7.1

Overall conversion rate is the ratio of people that went through the sales funnel to become buyers, against those that entered the funnel. This is normally expressed by a percentage of entrances. For example, a 70% conversion rate means that 70% of people that entered your funnel went on to purchase from you. This figure relies upon the in-process conversion rates we outlined above. Looking at Winter Parka again:

C= (CA * CI * CD *CAc)

C = (25% x 50% x 40% x 80%)

C = 3%

Another way to calculate the overall conversion rate is to use this formula:

C = (Conversions/Entrance) x 100

In Winter Parka's case,

C = (120/4000) x 100

C = 3%

While the latter is easier in calculating the overall conversion rate, the in-process conversion rates reveal more depth, areas where the sales funnel can be improved upon.

If Winter Parka spent $1,000 on their advertising campaign, had 4,000 people in Entrance, 120 buyers, and a 3% conversion rate; if no other costs were incurred by Winter Parka in this sales funnel, then the total cost expended to acquire one buyer is:

$1000/120 = $8.3

5.8 MARKETING VS SALES

Marketing and sales funnel terms are often used interchangeably, and attempting to distinguish between them can prove to be opaque. For the sake of consistency, and to avoid confusion, we have used the term 'sales funnel' throughout this book. However, much of our discussion arguably overlaps in marketing funnel territory. Using both terms would have complicated matters, in what is already a vast and difficult subject to comprehend at times. Having said that, it would be prudent to understand the difference, especially when you come across both terms in a different context.

The marketing funnel is focused on presenting a brand to an audience, to attract the attention of potential buyers, to persuade them into becoming prospects. This occurs by making them aware and develop a keen interest in your business. Once that occurs, and they enter the sales funnel, they become sales prospects.

On that basis, it would be correct to infer that the 4,000 visitors from Winter Parka who went from Entrance to Consideration constitute the marketing funnel. The sales funnel itself guides the prospects from Intent to Conversion, at which point they become buyers. The marketing and sales funnel work hand in hand to ensure that conversion takes place. Marketing builds interest, and the sales funnel itself is driven by marketing activity.

The marketing funnel plays a part in campaign strategy, driving awareness of products and services so that prospects have reasons to buy. The sales funnel takes the baton and looks to exploit those reasons, attempting to convince prospects to repeat their purchase, making them loyal customers and ultimately advocates.

Like the sales funnel, the marketing funnel is widest at the top and narrowest at the bottom, using a linear representation. At the top of the marketing funnel, it is important that your message strongly demonstrates a competitive advantage. This can be done in several ways, namely, marketing content (videos, articles, blog posts, and podcasts), creating referral programs, utilizing Search Engine Optimization (SEO), and using sponsored ads, to name a few. At this level, trying to strong-hand or coerce prospects into making urgent decisions will backfire, with mostly negative consequences.

To maximize conversions in the middle of the marketing funnel, you need to provide proof that your services are worth purchasing. Deliver specifications, technical details, and emphasise those reasons again for choosing you over your competitors. Use sponsored posts on social media platforms like Facebook and LinkedIn, and emails and newsletters to showcase guides, case studies, reports, and competitor comparisons tables. Never directly ask prospects to buy your products without giving them clear, concise, and distinguishable benefits.

The bottom part of the marketing funnel should be aimed at nudging prospects just that little bit further. Consider marketing channels such as sponsored posts, paid searches, customer testimonials, free trials, and demonstration requests. Do not go heavy on the text here or ask non-specific questions; that may kill the prospect's interest in what you have to offer.

5.9 NON-LINEAR FUNNELS

Currently, a debate has been raging amongst marketers as to whether the traditional linear marketing funnel is defunct, the argument being that modern consumers are increasingly entering the funnel at different stages. Because the average consumer or business is so much more knowledgeable than ever before, they are able to research and decide which brand, product, or service to opt for. Armed with so much prior knowledge, they enter the funnel at the Intent or Desire stages.

This is all due in part to the technological advances over the past decades. To put it simply, the internet happened, easing the way consumers can perform their research. As a result, customers can enter, exit, and dance around your sales funnel in any direction today. The stages at which the buyers enter the sales funnel is no longer indicative of where they are at their buyer's journey.

Particularly in the B2B environment, there are numerous touchpoints for an engagement at any given juncture, leading to an unpredictable and shorter sales cycle. It is therefore recommended that business personnel collaborate and explore strategies that cater to the non-linear journey, exploring ways to optimise the buyer experience. The funnel has arguably been transformed to include non-linear interactions across mediums like social media, email, and live chat. It is estimated that 80% of the groundwork is done by a business themselves, before they consider engagement with a sales representative.

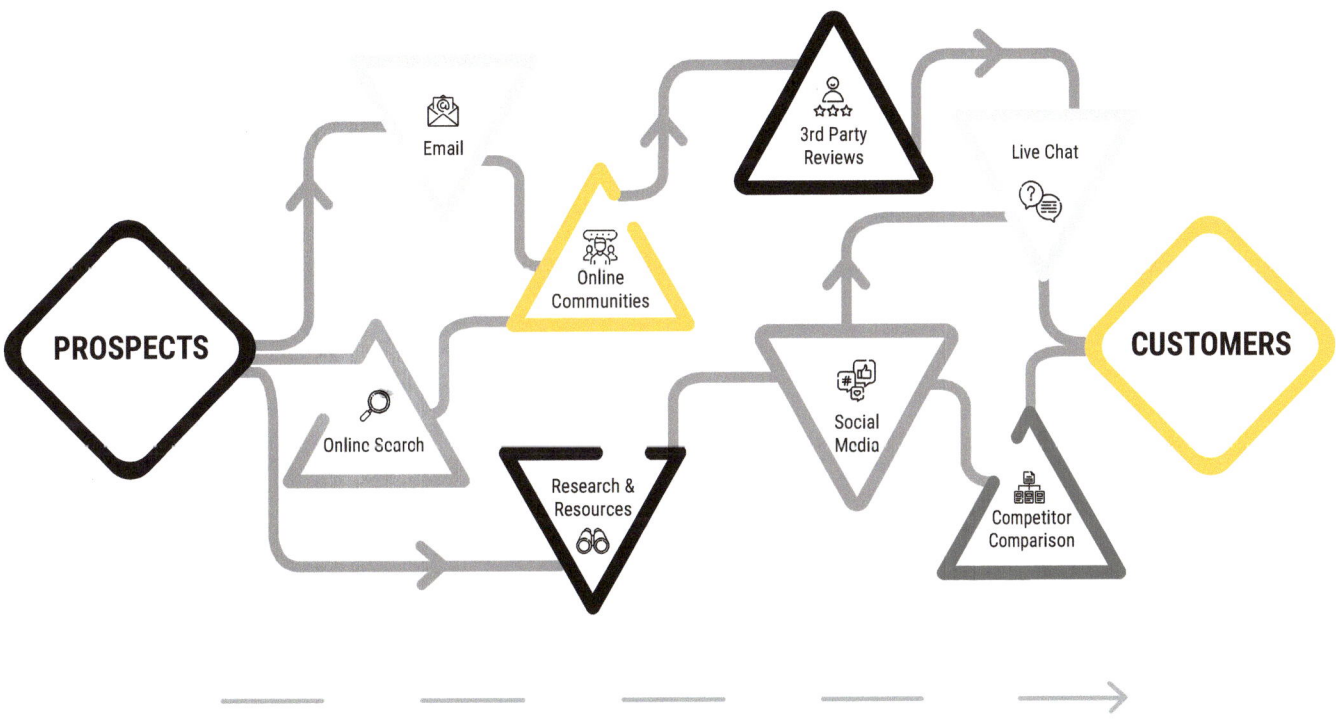

Regardless of stage, multiple entry points exist for Prospects to contact Sales through the buyer journey

Figure 5.9.1 – Non-linear sales funnel infographic

CHAPTER 5.0 SALES FUNNELS: A COMPREHENSIVE GUIDE

To survive in this environment business teams need to consider the following:

- Delivering the right content, to the right person, at the right time, and on the buyer's platform of choice.

- Marketing and sales teams need to collaborate in understanding which channels and content formats are preferred.

- Consider what time of day that prospective buyers are likely to take action.

- Develop personas for each of their key customer types. Use that to guide content marketing.

- Target content at the purchase, retention, advocacy, and re-engagement stages (Chapter 6.3).

- Mapping content against the buying journey of the ideal customer.

The non-linear approach is still fiercely debated amongst experts, take this quote from a Harvard Business Review article from 2014:

> **Brands may put the decision at the centre of the journey, but customers don't…"**
>
> – Mark Bonchek and Cara France

This leads to significant pressure on sales teams. They are in the position of having to cater to unpredictable interactions at any given moment, as well as dealing with the expectation of having their knowledge further enhanced. Add this to the fact that 74% of business buyers choose the first salesperson who added value to their search.

There is no agreed faultless model. So while it is wise to be aware of this alternative approach, the traditional linear buyer's journey and sales funnel remain the preferred choice of many marketers. However, as you will see, the non-linear model has a direct bearing in the e-commerce space.

5.10 FLIPPING THE FUNNEL

The reverse funnel is a process model commonly referred to as 'reverse marketing' or 'marketing backward.' Rather than start from the Entrance to create Awareness, the reverse sales funnel works backward from Advocacy to Entrance. Basically, it entails zeroing in on the desires of existing customers, discovering what makes them content, and then applying those parameters to prospects at various stages of the sales funnel. This results in customers starting to advocate on behalf of the business, which in turn, refuels the top of the marketing funnel by driving awareness and lead generation. When this happens, the sales funnel has effectively flipped – existing customers pulling prospects in, rather than the business pushing prospects through.

In order to achieve this, you need to identify a detailed persona for your ideal customer. To do that, answer this basic question: For **Whom** do I do **What**? Furthermore, you need to intimately understand the behaviour of this ideal customer, speak their language, what are their priorities, how do they expect delivery, when do they want it, and most importantly, why do they want it? Answering this honestly, objectively, and in detail will give you a clear picture of the traits, needs, and qualities of this ideal customer.

Once you are comfortable with this understanding, let that dictate your message, marketing content, media, and campaign strategy, all geared at targeting that ideal persona.

Let's consider 'flipped funnel' by stage, together with some techniques to realise them:

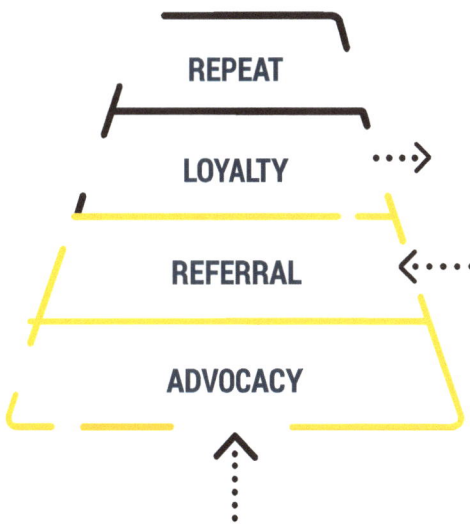

Figure 5.10.1 – The flipped funnel model

Repeat: Once a customer has purchased your product, the next step is to make them do it again! Persevere with bottom-funnel activities to encourage a repeat purchase.

- Post-purchase engagement – Reach out to your customer post-sale, such as a simple thank you email, requesting a social media follow or sharing relevant product-related content. The idea here is for them to keep you in mind, and want to return to your business.

- Second purchase incentive – Offer incentives, which is arguably the easiest way to a repeat purchase; "30% off your next purchase with this coupon code". However, think carefully about why you are doing this, and have a discount strategy in mind.

- Abandonment emails – Using those newly acquired web analysis skills, track when customers have come and gone. They are leaving you after having visited your website again, or left a product in your cart. Follow up emails with a "just a reminder you left this product in your cart" will help. Maybe offering that second purchase incentive here might be a good strategy.

Loyalty: At this stage, the customer becomes preferential to your products. In turn, customers develop a preference for your brand, beginning to associate with it, and nurture your products. Engagement is the key here, and you can cultivate their connection with your brand through community development and outreach.

- **Loyalty programmes** – This is a tried and tested method that perpetuates long-term customer engagement and repeat buying. But remember, you need to offer rewards for this commitment, be this through discounts, privileged access, or some sort of points-based system that they can spend in kind.

- **Customer service** – Make this a priority! Provide a service that exemplifies patience, empathy, and clear communication, among others. Do not underestimate the importance customers place on good customer service. A negative experience, not only impacts their custom, but also your brand.

- **Personalized content and product recommendations** – Studies have shown that customers are willing to pay a premium if it means they receive personalised content. Offer recommendations from what you know about them. Using this to send to them personalised offers or content.

- **Beyond the product or service** – Provide them with an exclusive view into your business by demonstrating another side. Examples include high-value educations posts or a peek into your day-to-day operations.

- **Multiple channels for communication** – Make it clear that you're easily available across more than one channel – be that email, phone, or social media. Ideally, if you have the resources through 24/7 methods, such as round the clock live chat. All this provides a positive brand experience and lets customers easily comment, feedback, and query.

Referral: Once you have gained their loyalty, the customer is more likely to refer you to others and recommend your products and services to them.

- **Referral schemes** – In this system, you incentivise your current customers to refer new people to your business. Offer rewards such as discounts, small gifts, or special offers for every successful referral.

Advocacy: This is the ultimate evolution for nurturing existing customers. When they write good product reviews about you and post about your products on social media, they help to drive more leads for your marketing and sales funnel. Work here to develop better communities that can support and advocate for your brand.

- **Actively seek out your advocates** – Obtain feedback from customers regularly. For example, request a 1 – 10 rating of whether they would recommend you to friends, family, or colleagues. Those that give you a 9 or 10 rating are potential advocates.

- **Nurture them** – It's simple – give them all the support they need to continue doing what they are doing. Be careful that this does not overlap into the realms of sponsored advocacy. Nothing is more powerful to a prospect's decision-making than seeing an independent party advocating your brand, product, or services.

Finally, track your results. If you are seeing an increase in what you perceive to be the ideal customer, then your understanding has been validated. If not, focus again on your successful engagements to teach you what you are doing right and what needs to be adjusted. Do not sit on your laurels if all bodes well, but rather think of it as an incremental process of refinement.

Experiment, test, feedback, and refinement should be your mantra throughout your digital marketing journey.

6.0 THE ONLINE SALES FUNNEL

To recap, the sales funnel is the route your customers take from first becoming aware of your brand to making a purchase. As you would expect, the online sales funnel is no different in that respect. It exists on the same principles that we have discussed thus far – tracking the buyer journey from visitor, prospect to customer, followed by a pursuit of repeat business, loyalty, and advocacy. Or awareness, nurture, convert, and delight. However, the online marketplace is where we start to see real change to this approach.

You have seen how the sales funnel has a wide top. This is based on the premise that attention is abundant. When the sales funnel was envisaged in 1898, this was certainly the case. Post a flyer through someone's door over 10 years, there is a strong chance that eventually they will look at it. However, today we live in a time where everyone has access to multiple media channels and information is profusely available and attention readily obtainable. The mass blitzing approach is not as effective as it used to be.

To cater this new information model, we will discuss how the sales funnel has evolved online, exactly what this new model looks like, its various incarnations, techniques for managing churn, the impact of SEO, and why you need to adapt to survive.

> " **Leads have increasingly started to enter the sales funnel at any point.**

6.1 THE FUNNEL IS EVOLVING

Mr St. Elmo's purchase model from way back in 1898 has been the de-facto guide for marketers for nearly 100 years. What this proves is that the initial concept was indeed a brilliant idea. But as we have seen, emerging media, technology, and changing modes of marketing have led to variations on this original theme.

The internet did not entirely erase everything from the past; it only upended them enough to expand the basic AIDA model. This, in turn, gave birth to the online or digital sales funnel, a process more focused on a non-linear model in terms of education and brand engagement, and embracing of the online customer shopping experience.

The age-old method of acquiring visitors through ad banners is giving way to marketing content through social media and other channels. As a result, buyers are free to choose their paths. For example, by conducting their research, reading consumer choice reports, and checking reviews, a person may enter the sales funnel at the Purchase stage and go from there straight to being a brand Advocate.

Leads have increasingly started to enter the sales funnel at any point. If you recall, it was this school of thought that gave rise to the non-linear model in the first place. The basic AIDA model has evolved to include more stages such as Engagement, Education, and Research, in some cases, employing the flipped model. All of which we shall discuss in detail in the following chapters.

Changes in the buyer's journey and the many wonders of the internet, have also led to accessible ways for marketers to enter the customer journey at different stages. They are finding themselves needing to focus on creative ways to market visitors, prospects, and customers, through more direct reach than they ever had before.

CHAPTER 6.0 THE ONLINE SALES FUNNEL

6.2 THE NEW ONLINE MODEL

Even with all the changes that the online model has spawned, marketers are still required to perform their routine job of attracting leads, generating interest, engagement, prompting decisions, and action. With the caveat that it is not necessarily in this order, nor is it using the same methods as before. The marketers' job now is to cater to potential customers at every stage.

As we have seen the funnel can be "flipped" or even likened to a "loop". Catering to the broader context of the buying experience. Allowing for avenues in the post-sales period, generating repeat customers and brand advocates. Hence, the new model encourages a more rounded approach to marketing, taking into account the entire customer lifecycle.

All this means that today's sales funnel requires an omnichannel approach. i.e., integrating different methods of shopping available, such as onsite, social, mobile, email, physical, and instant messaging. You need to remove the boundaries between the sales and marketing channels to create a unified, integrated whole. Instead of the product being at the centre, it is the customer. You should merge the worlds of websites, emails, retargeted ads, social media marketing, and physical locations to show personalized offers, products, and messages. To demonstrate, let's run with an extensive Winter Parka scenario:

I. A <u>prospect</u> goes through the process of completing the buyers' form in the hope of purchasing a coat, but for whatever reason fails to complete it. He leaves without purchasing.

II. Winter Parka sends the prospect an email promotion "$25 off their next purchase." However, this is ignored by the prospect.

III. At the same time, the prospect is served ads for both the coat and the promotional offer on Facebook, Pinterest, Instagram, and YouTube, which are staggered over a week so as not to appear overbearing.

IV. Following a week of no uptake, Winter Parka changes its approach by serving ads highlighting its ethical environmental policy and work with Alaskan wildlife trusts, each with a Call To Action (CTA), requesting the prospect to view its Environmental Activity web page.

V. A YouTube ad featuring their wildlife preservation trust finally prompts engagement.

VI. After viewing another video, the prospect decides to launch winterparka.inc and browse their new winter coat 'Fall Collection.'

VII. Soon after, Winter Parka targets the prospect with a new round of ads promoting the 'Fall Collection', together with an increased promotional offer of $35.

CHAPTER 6.0 THE ONLINE SALES FUNNEL

VIII. Intrigued, the prospect clicks the ad and selects a particular coat, completes the buyer form, but then changes their mind again, thinking that it would be best to go and try a coat for size before purchasing it online.

IX. Winter Parka anticipates this and detects the prospect's address is near an Anchorage outlet.

X. A few days, later the prospect receives a personalised letter in the post to try out their fall collection at the local Anchorage outlet.

XI. The prospect submits, visiting the local outlet, trying on the coat they had been eyeing up online and buys. Incidentally, upon purchase they use the Point of Sale (POS) system in the outlet, updating their account details in the process.

XII. Upon arriving home, the customer receives a "Thank you" email and a week later receives another requesting a product review.

XIII. The customer chooses not to act on the email request; however, as the customer is following Winter Parka on Instagram, they receive another product review request via the messenger service.

XIV. The customer feels obligated to leave a quick positive review, as it's so convenient and quick through the messaging service.

XV. Winter Parka notes the last two positive touchpoints and therefore sends the customer a "Refer a Friend" promotional offer email the following week.

XVI. Facebook, Pinterest, Instagram, and YouTube promotion ads have now all ceased for the customer. They are replaced by promotional activity that is staggered over a longer period.

XVII. Sometime after, much to Winter Parka's delight, the customer purchased two further coats. This triggers an auto-responding email campaign, as well as ads across their social media.

XVIII. The customer chooses to ignore the ads, but Winter Parka notices the customer's activity on their environmental activity page again.

XIX. The next email and social media ads directly reference this interest.

While this may seem somewhat elaborate, all this is completely feasible with today's digital technology and actively practice, in most cases, maybe not to the extent we have shown, but certain variations and subsets thereof. As you can see, there are multiple touchpoints and the customer remains the focal point in all the marketing activity. The customer's behaviour initiates the strategy, nothing here is random. Instead, there is full alignment with customer behaviour and between channels.

To deliver a consistent and effective brand message this does require multiple departments to work together, marketing, sales, product, and customer support. Each department needs to appreciate the goals and objectives of the campaigns, allowing for a more cohesive user experience across all your communication channels.

As we mentioned, the impact to the funnel is for it to be "flipped", "looped" or variations thereof. What this means is what we shall explore next.

6.3 ONLINE FUNNEL TYPES

No two buyers' journeys are the same; each journey arguably creates its own funnel type. As a result, there are several types of online funnels. Listed below are three of the most known and well-used in modern sales.

6.3.1 The Hourglass Online Funnel

As its name denotes, this funnel resembles an hourglass, focuses on the non-linear experience, and consists of up to 10 steps. A more detailed approach to the journey is taken here, stressing the importance of cultivating and sustaining relationships with customers. There is a great deal more attention paid to each user, by asking the marketer to pay heed to a better experience for the target audience.

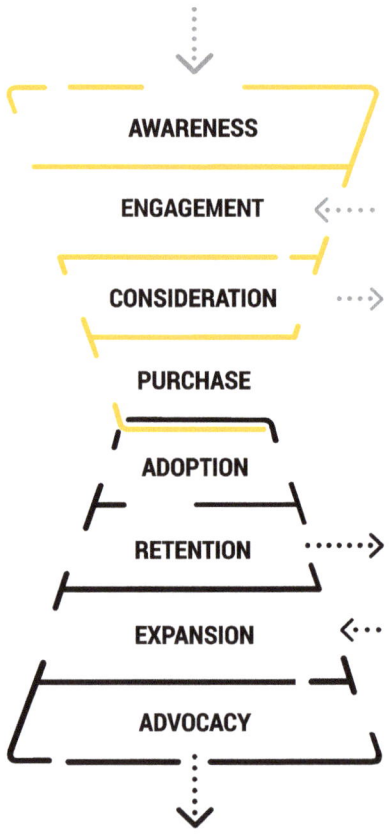

Figure 6.3.1 – The Hourglass Online Funnel

Enter Harry, a Winter Parka prospect. Before he actually bought a coat from them, he underwent several pre-purchase stages:

Engagement: Becomes aware of the products and services through advertising campaigns, brand awareness initiatives.

Education: Identifies the fact that he has a problem. Winter is coming, and he has no coat to withstand a strong blizzard.

Research: Discovers a solution. Reads a Winter Parka blog on a 3 nylon fabric that is proven to be exceptionally effective in arctic conditions.

Evaluation: Viewing their website product catalogue, he discovers the range of coats, sizes, and colours he is fond of and all within budget.

Justification: The money makes sense, the coat has all the qualities he's after. What's not to like?

Purchase: Takes the plunge and becomes a customer. Purchasing online using a quick and simple sales process.

Followed by these post-purchase stages:

Adoption: As forecast, a particularly cold blizzard arrives in Anchorage and Harry wears his coat on his daily commute to work. He is satisfied with his pre-emptive purchase.

Retention: Winter Parka reaches out to Harry for social media follows. Harry is impressed with their environmental credentials and fun imagery. He decides to follow, developing a connection with the brand.

Expansion: Winter Parka sends promotional emails of related products such as scarves, gloves, and boots, prompting Harry to think about an additional purchase to replace some worn boots.

Advocacy: Impressed with himself, having purchased something of such quality at this price range and feeling connected with the brand, Harry has no hesitation in telling his friends and family of his purchases and customer experience.

Harry's stages after purchase are linear, but the pre-purchase stages could have admitted him at any time. For example, he may have discovered his lack of winter protection before being made aware of the Winter Parka brand.

6.3.2 Looping Online Funnel

In contrast to the Hourglass Online Funnel, the Looping Funnel is less-organized and more flexible, allowing every user to have their own distinct buyer's journey. It features six stages:

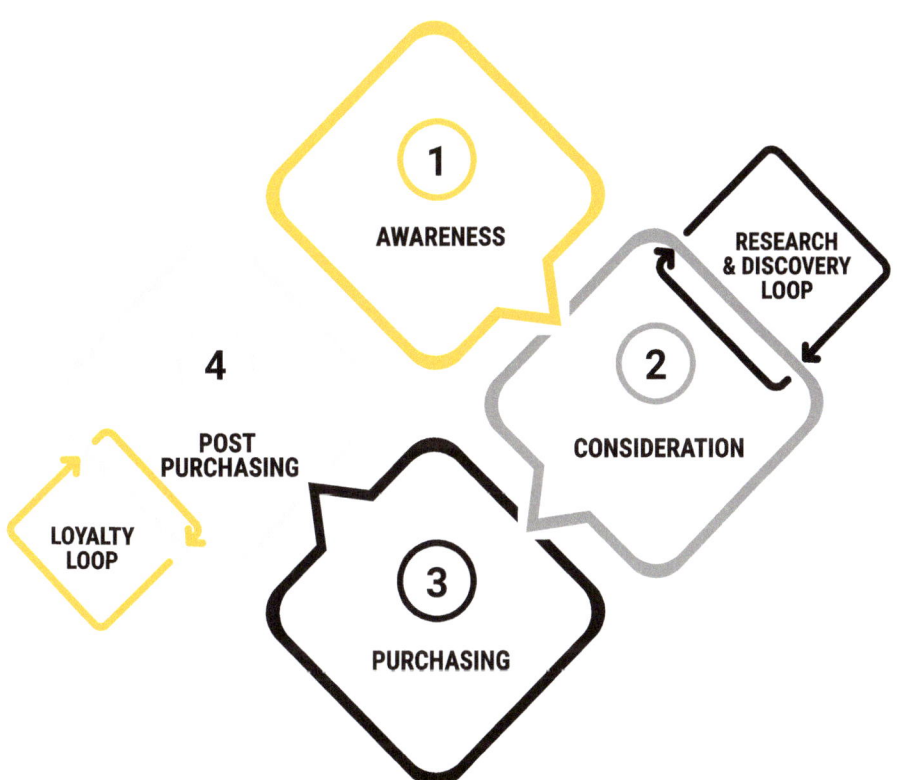

Figure 6.3.2 – Looping Online Funnel

The Looping online funnel is flexible and can be used for any kind of business in any industry. It can also be tailored to meet specific needs. For example, adding an Intent stage before Purchase or placing more focus on the Loyalty stage. It is simple but very adaptable and effective in aligning itself with the online shopping experience.

Let's delve into the stages of the looping funnel, with our old friend Harry:

Awareness: Identifies the fact that he has a problem. Winter is coming, and he has no coat to withstand a strong blizzard.

Consideration: Discovers a solution. Reads up online on a 3 nylon fabric that is proven to be exceptionally effective in arctic conditions.

Research and Discovery Loop: Goes online to research and finds several brands selling winter coats. However, Winter Parka has a great selection of that nylon fabric he's after, within his price range and he likes their environmental credentials.

Purchase: He decides to proceed with a purchase from Winter Parka.

Post-Purchase Experience: Winter Parka reaches out to him offering 35% off his next purchase, and details of their referral program.

Loyalty Loop: Harry takes up the promotional offer and purchases some winter boots with the 35% discount. Being a loyal customer, Winter Parka provides him with a free woollen beanie hat.

6.3.3 Micro-Moments Online Funnel

> **Micro-moment**
>
> – *Noun: An intent-rich moment when a person turns to a device to act on a need to know, go, do or buy.*

This funnel takes its inspiration from Google's micro-moments.[b] It focuses on the impetus that drives a user into entering the funnel, from the marketer or business's point of view.

From a Winter Parka perspective, here is how this works:

- **Want-to-Know Moment**: Harry explores what kind of winter coats are available at his price range.

"When someone is exploring or researching, but it is not necessarily in purchase mode."

- **Want-to-Do Moment**: Harry wants to know what the most effective fabrics for arctic conditions are.

"When someone wants help completing a task or trying something new."

- **Want-to-Go Moment**: Where and how far is my nearest winter clothing store, what are their opening times, and do they have the kind of coat I want in stock?

"When someone is looking for a local business or is considering buying a product at a nearby store."

- **Want-to-Buy Moment**: Harry has done his research, is armed with the knowledge of fabric, size, and price, and he is now ready to explore brands and purchase.

"When someone is ready to make a purchase and may need help deciding what to buy or how to buy it."

This funnel does not follow the actions of customers and users. Instead, business owners need to figure out what their prospects are likely to do in one of these micro-moments. It is then up to the business to collaborate and brainstorm ideas to accommodate these needs. What that response looks like will articulate your funnel.

For example, let's consider the **Want-to-Go Moment** further:

Our friend Harry is intent on visiting a local winter clothing store as he likes to try before purchasing. He performs online research for local winter clothing outlets. It is up to Winter Parka to ensure they have a strong chance of featuring in any searches Harry performs. Their store details, opening times, and any promotions they are currently running must be listed in Harry's search results in some shape or form. Digging deeper, they are aware 82% of their customers say that they use their mobile to search for a local business. So they are particularly optimised for mobiles, providing an easy to navigate and clear web experience, thereby nudging the customer a little further in the Consideration stage.

In essence, your job here as a marketer is to build strong "be there" moments across all these four key micro-moments, leading you to formulate a sales funnel for each one.

For more information please visit:

https://www.thinkwithgoogle.com/consumer-insights/consumer-journey/micro-moments-understand-new-consumer-behavior/

7.0 PLUGGING THE LEAK

Linear or non-linear, regardless of your funnel type, all are prone to leaking. Some people are not interested; others never buy. This is, in part, the normal course of marketing and sales. When you need to be concerned is when there is excessive leaking. We saw in Chapter 5.4 (Benefits of the Funnel) that there are numerous advantages in mapping your buyer journey. The key advantage is being able to track drop off – exactly what stage are people leaving disproportionately and why?

If you recall, Winter Parka had only 40% of their visitors convert from Interest to Desire (See Table 5.5.1). This should be an area where the company needs to focus on. Why is it that so many people were considering them, and then dropped off? What are the competitors doing in terms of marketing or product that are enticing 60% of their visitors? Fortunately, there are measures you can take to ensure such leaks are plugged. The fundamental ones will be discussed here in detail.

7.1 METRICS

As you build your funnel, you must assign clear and concise metrics to each stage. These will enable you to track and measure progress against several factors, such as cost, visits, clicks, etc., and all are readily available in most web analytical tools. Here are some typically found in the key stages:

Awareness: Number of people that are visiting your website in a given period, be it on your landing or any page for that matter. Web analytical tools will be able to identify unique visitors from all your traffic.

Interest: Number of people that subscribed to your website in a given period. For example, registering for your newsletter or email list.

Desire: Click-through-rate – The number of impressions a marketing campaign has made in a given cycle. This could be emails read, online ads clicked or social media video ads played, to name a few.

Action: Number of people that finally purchased your products. Conversion rate, how many went on to actually fully transact as a proportion of those that were targeted.

It is fundamental for your funnel to be actively measuring these metrics cyclically, by campaign activity, or both. Where you notice variations to the norm, such as a sharp decline, you know you have an issue requiring further investigation, such as a dip post-Christmas, impact on a particular channel, or suddenly ranking poorly with your keywords. While you may not be able to pinpoint where the issue is immediately, having those numbers at hand is an easy place to begin searching for the root cause, and then you can look at identifying ways to resolve the issue.

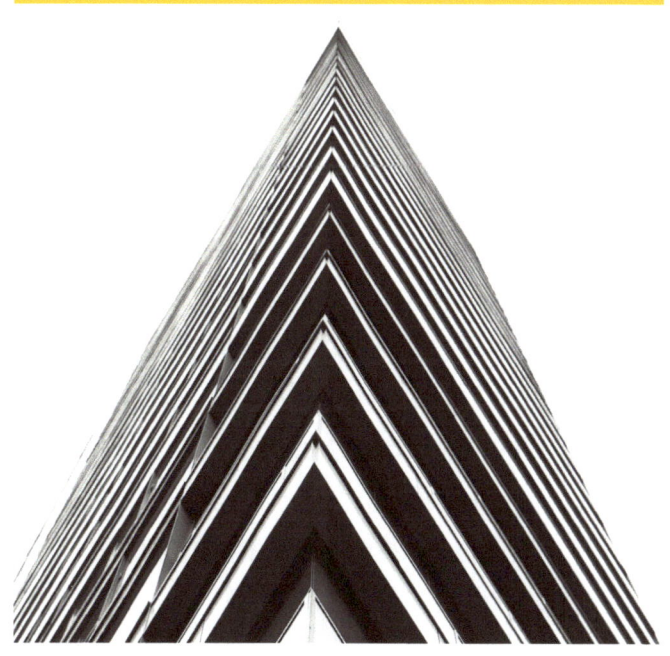

CHAPTER 7.0 LUGGING THE LEAK

7.1.1 Key Performance Indicators

Key Performance Indicator, or KPI's as they are commonly referred to, are metrics that are used to quantify progress towards a business objective. In the context of the sales funnel, these are important in determining checkpoints towards specific goals you set for your funnel. How do you know which metric is a KPI? Ask yourself "Can I improve this metric and still fail to meet my set objective"? If the answer is "yes", then you have a leading indicator rather than a KPI.

> **Output Metrics** – A measure of your activity or output for a specific period.
>
> E.g., the number of videos you create on your YouTube channel for a specific period.
>
> **Outcome Metrics** – A measure of the impact of your Output metrics. The extent of influence your output is having as an indication of performance.

E.g., the number of views your videos are having on your YouTube channel.

Such metrics are also commonly referred to as **leading** and **lagging** indicators. Lead indicators give you an insight into future performance and lagging indicators measure actual results. Following on from our example above, lead indicators would be the number of views your YouTube video generates, whereas the lagging indicator would be the actual number of YouTube subscribers you are acquiring.

All of which amounts to areas in the funnel that require focus to meet your set objectives and identify stages that are proving problematic. Below we list some common leading and lagging indicators you can use to track your goals:

Driving Website Traffic

Website Sessions – Lagging indicator, providing a total number of visits to your website, which includes new and repeat visits. Probably the single most important KPI for driving traffic to your website. Corresponding lead indicator example: Number of blog posts published.

New Users – Number of new visitors to your website. Important in that it is a clear indication of how successful you are in driving new traffic to your website. Corresponding leading indicator example: Number of Facebook Ad campaigns.

Organic Clicks – Refers to the number of clicks in a search results page that have nothing to do with any paid search. An excellent indicator of your SEO efforts. If your clicks are down then you need further optimisation for search keywords. Corresponding leading indicator example: New external followed links earned.

> **How do you know which metric is a KPI? Ask yourself "Can I improve this metric and still fail to meet my set objective"? If the answer is "yes", then you have a leading indicator rather than a KPI.**

Increasing Brand Loyalty2

Repeat Visitors – Visitors who repeatedly viewed your website. Such visitors are more likely to proceed down your sales funnel. Hence, this is an important metric to help you track performance. Work to increase this metric volume. Corresponding leading indicator example: Number of emails sent in a campaign.

Branded Search Volume – Is an indication of people who are searching using keywords that can be directly associated with your brand, allowing you to determine how strong your brand awareness is. Corresponding leading indicator example: Number of paid display advertising impressions.

Impressions – The number of times your site appears in search results and was viewed by users. Another great indicator of brand awareness and in turn, how effective your SEO efforts are. Corresponding leading indicator example: Number of articles you published in your newsletter.

Growing Community Engagement

Social Group Engagement – Refers to the number of members who are actively participating in your branded groups, such as Facebook or LinkedIn. Active interaction is a great indication that your brand community is shaping up to become strong, loyal, and growing. Corresponding leading indicator example: Number of social media posts published.

Social Engagements – The act of interaction by your followers on social media, be that through follows, likes, comments, shares, etc. There is more value in engaging followers than just simply having a large amount of them, as these followers are likely to step through your sales funnel. Corresponding leading indicator example: Quality of social media posts published.

User-Generated Content (UGC) – Unpaid branded content posted by your followers, in the hope that you will go on to post to *your* social media. The value in this metric lies in the exposure it provides to new audiences and in determining how engaged your customers are with your brand. Corresponding leading indicator example: Number of campaigns seeking UGC.

Sales Team Qualified Leads

Marketing Qualified Leads (MQL) – Heavily engaged contacts, such as those who have downloaded your eBook or registered for your newsletter. This metric should be tracked to ensure the sales team has a constant stream of leads to follow-up on and actively entering the top of the funnel. Corresponding leading indicator example: Number of blog posts published on your newsletter.

Number of Leads – A person or business is identified as a potential lead. You need to set well-defined lead goals for your funnels, measure them, and maintain progress. If you're lacking leads, then re-visit your marketing strategy. Your funnel will let you know. Corresponding leading indicator example: Number of advertising campaigns conducted for a period.

Number of Booked Meetings – Keeping an eye on sales meetings booked will help identify the quality of your leads. Having a large number of leads will mean nothing if you're only booking a handful of meetings from them. It may be indicating that you need to address your marketing strategy and target audience. Corresponding leading indicator example: Number of sales calls made.

CHAPTER 7.0 LUGGING THE LEAK

Improving Lead Qualification

Time to Response – Days, hours, or minutes. This metric is a measure of how long you are typically taking for a sales response to a lead. Delays can be a cause for churn and this is a great tool to enable your team's communication to be more efficient. Corresponding leading indicator example: Number of sales representatives.

Number of Logged Emails – A measure of the number of emails logged with your Customer Relationship Management System (CRM). To move leads down the sales funnel, communication needs to be happening throughout each stage. Monitoring the number of emails logged provides sales an indication of potential customer numbers. Corresponding leading indicator example: Number of contacts in the CRM.

Deals Created – One of the most important KPI's is tracking how many deals are being created in a given period. Marketing and sales have one ultimate goal in mind, closing deals to generate money. Tracking this metric provides you with the means to see how successful your marketing and sales efforts are.

Maintaining Current Customers

Retention/Churn Rate – In terms of retention, it is the number of customers that return to you to do business. Regarding churn, it is the percentage of customers that you have lost from the same period. Together they should add up to 100%. For example, 90% retention, means 10% churn. The value is the insight it provides of customer satisfaction and brand loyalty. Corresponding leading indicator example: Number of daily active users.

Net Promoter Score – A quantitative measure of customer loyalty. Normally determined through a survey or brief question such as "on a scale of 1 – 10, how likely are you to recommend us to a friend?". Repeated poor scoring reflects poor brand loyalty and a need to address marketing and brand awareness. Corresponding leading indicator example: Support ticket response time.

Average Life Time Value – Is a measure of the revenue a typical customer is likely to generate through the average customer lifetime. It allows you to gauge the average customer to your business and how they are tracking over time. Helps you determine the most valuable customers in your business. Corresponding leading indicator example: Number of emails sent in a marketing campaign.

The key idea here is to set your business objectives/goals first and let that dictate which KPI's you should be tracking.

7.1.2 More Than The Metrics

As a digital marketer, you should be well aware by now of how data is critical to driving strategy and decisions. Whilst this is true, you should not overlook human behaviour and remain overtly committed to data. Consider the following in determining your target market and business objectives:

User Intent – Build an online experience that will keep users moving through your funnel. Carefully consider the user intent. For example, someone looking to find a car service shop is typically looking for information such as prices by model, location details, the opening hours, and how to book. In turn, the shop ensures all this information features in their Google Ads, website, and My Business page on Google, so that all this is visible in search results pages.

User Interactions – Consider how people are engaging with your business, both online and offline; it will provide you with an insight of what works and what does not. For example, you may find that your target audience is particularly responsive to video marketing. In which case, you then decide to set up a YouTube channel that better showcases your products and services.

Revenue – This is integral to measuring the success of your sales funnel. Focus on the money that has been generated as a direct result of all that marketing activity. While you may have earned a ton of conversions from your most recent ad campaign, it was for low-cost products. For your company, that resulted in less revenue. It also led to a low-performing campaign that failed to deliver a return. Explore the analytics of your campaign, but also look at the results it had on your business.

Gross Margin – Revenue does not account for the cost of goods. It is therefore imperative that

you assess your gross margin for a specific period. This is a determination of how much revenue your business retains. Much like revenue, this will enable you to gauge the success of your sales funnel and provide you with further insight. However other factors will have an impact here and need to be considered, such as under-priced products to move inventory. However, this does not reflect a poor sales funnel, but rather a poor pricing model.

Profit – To be considered in terms of digital marketing. Ultimately you want to see what sort of return your marketing efforts are making. Profit can demonstrate exactly what sort of impact your activities are having on the bottom line. It can also be used to direct your sales funnel activity, example, directing your marketing efforts to an audience who have proven to be the most profitable.

7.2 Search Engine Optimisation (SEO)

 the practice of increasing the quantity and quality of traffic to your website through organic search engine results"

Throughout this book, we have come across the SEO term several times. But exactly what is it and how does it impact your sales funnel, particularly as a tool for plugging those leaks.

By definition, SEO is the practice of increasing the quantity and quality of traffic to your website through organic search engine results, i.e., ranking well for quality searches on result pages (SERPs). There is no point in ranking well for an Apple Computer search when your business is to be selling the fruit. Beyond this, ranking well in SERPs means more traffic, leading to more opportunities, conversions, and brand awareness. Critical to all this are keywords – words that are well-researched and are responsible for featuring you on SERPs. In a digital marketing context, it is these keywords that then go on to be featured in marketing campaigns, content, websites, and blogs.

As we have seen, SEO plays a major role in helping the sales funnel at various stages. In aggregate, we can look at certain types of keyword searches that target content at different stages of the funnel. Some keyword types are better at awareness building for most searches; while other keywords signal an intent to purchase. Let's explore the impact of SEO on the key stages:

Awareness – This would appear to be the most obvious stage for SEO. A shopper performs a search for a product on Google (other search engines apply) your website appears on the SERP. It is the first time the shopper has come across your business. This is a chance to seed that awareness; at this stage it's about information and the keywords the shopper is using is an entry into that awareness. Your keywords at this stage should be product-centric – informational or educational, resulting in your business appearing before the shopper, generating awareness of your product or brand.

Product category keywords on the other hand would drive traffic to your home or product category pages. Whereas the more specific ones should lead directly to your product pages, for example, "men's shoes" as opposed to "men's leather hiking boots." Therefore, expect to identify different keywords for different page groups.

Intent and Desire – Interception searches are the key here, with the goal of driving traffic to the middle of the funnel. Such keywords are slightly longer and specific than the awareness ones. The shopper may use modifiers such as size, colour, or brand. For example "men's leather hiking boots size 10." This demonstrates the shopper's desire to narrow in on the purchase, but he/she is not quite ready to purchase yet. This could also be said of those searches that contain the word "review."

Action – Keywords with specific product names, numbers, or attributes signal a desire to purchase. These shoppers come armed with a lot more knowledge; they know exactly what they want and where they are going to buy it. As a result, the search activity is more about narrowing in on the best site to buy. For example, "Timberland brown men's leather hiking boots UK size 10." These would obviously be the best keywords for you to feature in; however, they will prove difficult to optimise because of the numerous permutations for a given product. However, there are techniques to capture these keywords at scale by using highly optimized product pages that contain many product details.

Determining which keywords sit at which levels of the funnel is subjective and relative. It's subjective in that the same 100 keywords could apply to different categories; it's relative in that an awareness-driver on one site could be an action-driver for another, depending on the business model. Align those keywords with the three areas of the funnel that SEO can drive traffic to, and then make sure you have content that fills the needs of each of those areas.

7.3 Retargeting

So, you have spent $1,000 on paid advertising for an eBook to generate sales for your product website. Much to your disappointment, while 300 visitors have downloaded the eBook, it has resulted in zero sales for your products. Although, what you now have is an opportunity to retarget those 300 visitors. Retargeting is a technique whereby you aim to reacquire those visitors and lure them back into your sales funnel. This is typically done by installing a small amount of JavaScript code known as 'pixel' on your website. It works by dropping cookies into the visitors' browser so that even when the visitor leaves your website, they are still shown your ads on advertising platforms such as Facebook, Google, Quora, and the like. Businesses can access pixels quite easily. Most advertising platforms allow users to generate pixels, which are then added to the header section of the website.

The challenging part of the retargeting process is to know what kind of content to re-display. The good news is the sales funnel is here to help you. Knowing where your visitors are dropping

> **" a technique whereby you aim to reacquire those visitors and lure them back into your sales funnel.**

off, enables you to plan your retargeting with a display ad for the next stage in the funnel. For example, display a promotional ad to those 300 who downloaded your eBook with a product promotional offer by way of thanks. Once you have this perfectly in play, it can be extended to retargeting campaigns, aimed at every stage of the funnel, with appropriate offers for the next stage.

7.4 Live Chat

People sometimes leave websites because they can't find the information they are looking for. Information such as reading your product description, but failing to obtain the clarification they were seeking, or having questions on the packaging and delivery you have to offer. With readily available online competitors, keeping the visitor on your site is paramount. This is where live chat can come in, where you aid the visitor with any questions they have with an immediate response.

Regardless of where your visitor is in your sales funnel, with live chat you now have the means to address any queries and gently nudge them to the next stage. All this has the added advantage of doubling as a lead generator, as most live chat platforms require contact information to converse. With tools like Intercom.com, you can also segment visitors accordingly, sending them an automated message, encourage them to the next step in your funnel. Identify what are the most common questions about your product or service and have these directly addressed in your live chat.

7.5 Artificial Intelligence (AI) & Machine Learning

Using AI software to analyse large amounts of data can help your business make campaign improvements fast. Amongst the ways such software can help include:

- Personalising user experiences.
- Predicting user intent.
- Drawing connections between separate pieces of data, like user behaviour and business goals.
- Discovering keyword and content opportunities.

The ability to collect data, analyse, apply, and learn from it is powerful and for that matter, leading change in digital marketing. Brands such as Amazon and Spotify are actively using AI systems to manage their marketing strategy. Consider some areas where AI is having an impact:

Customer Relationship Management (CRM) – Combining CRM with AI maximises user data collection from different platforms, develops shrewd customer insight, and determines user needs in the process. Customer behavioural information becomes a great source of AI analysis. E.g., product purchase pages that are being viewed, and tools that are most commonly being used. AI analysis provides enhanced visualization of the customer journey, which in turn will refine your sales funnel.

AI Chatbots – In recent years, AI-based customer service has become increasingly common and available to businesses. The development of better AI semantic recognition, language processing, and voice conversion has spearheaded this evolution. The main advantages are being able to service multiple customers and providing support 24/7 across time zones. Many well-known brands are increasingly using AI chatbots implemented with existing messenger services such as WhatsApp, Facebook Messenger, and Slack. Many companies now offer AI chatbot services for small businesses, making it one of the more accessible AI technologies.

Email Marketing – With the help of AI technology, user behaviour can be used to prepare personalised email marketing campaigns. Allowing marketers to automatically trigger emails through defined actions such as cart abandonment, feedback and loyalty emails. Sending personalised email to the customer inbox with relevant subject lines, product recommendations, and customer details. All of this can stem from customer behaviour. AI in this context can also be used for campaign analysis. Rather than having to conduct lengthy A/B testing yourself, AI can analyse and optimise campaigns in a far shorter time. This is also a relatively mature technology in the digital marketing sphere, and relatively affordable through service providers such as Phrasee and Seventh Sense.

Marketing Content – Based on customer behaviour analysis, the power of AI can easily determine which content is most effective, arming the marketer with knowledge of what content gets results. Sharing and creating the right form of content. It's not just in content analysis where AI is making in-roads, content creation is also becoming a factor. Tools such as FlexClip video maker allow you to create and download high-quality videos, with no need for a designer or technical skills for that matter. If your analysis dictates that video content is the most effective, then such a tool gets you to market quickly. Finally, curation is another factor that you should be aware of. You may have come across Amazon product recommendations on your account, learning from previous purchases and your buying habits. Based on your customer engagement, a similar tactic can be utilised by your small business to recommend blogs, products, videos, etc. Tools such as Freshrelevance.com and Recombee are readily available to implement recommendation engines in your online presence.

Whilst this all sounds ideal, it does come at a cost, a very high one. To develop your own AI and machine learning, the costs are astronomical, as the computing power required behind the software is significantly high and the algorithms themselves particularly complex. However, there are software companies that will provide SaaS-based services, such as Blueshift and Albert AI, but again they are not cheap. If you can afford it, the rewards should easily outweigh your cost in time, if suitably utilised to enhance your sales funnel. If you cannot, then it would be prudent to be aware of this evolving technology as it becomes more widespread in digital marketing and costs will slowly come down.

CHAPTER 7.0 LUGGING THE LEAK

7.6 **A Quick Reference Guide**

	SEO	Email	Content	Social Media
TOP FUNNEL	Exploratory keywords – cater for early-stage problem searches. E.g. "common winter flowers for gardens" or "budget android phone reviews".	Provide high-quality value to register visitor email addresses. E.g. "free eBook download." No sale activity at this stage.	User-focused content strategy, optimised for prospect research. E.g. "blogs, infographics, videos, podcasts."	Showcase your business and products to develop good brand awareness across customer social platforms.
MIDDLE FUNNEL	Target keywords that naturally flow from initial searches. Namely, informational searches. E.g. "where can I buy winter flowers near me" or "best electrical stores".	Motivate your subscribers with offers such as promotions, exclusive content, and updates.	Create content that answers those "why" questions. In-depth content such as guides and webinars. Content should be gated, information in exchange for prospect information.	Generate engaging content for your followers. E.g. "contests and social posts".
BOTTOM FUNNEL	Focus on actionable high-value keywords featuring "buy". Feature these in any Pay Per Click (PPC) ad campaigns. E.g. "buy 75-inch TV".	Target a segmented audience, such as those ready for pre-ordering, or abandoned carts being sent a reminder email. Consider intent and how that should exist in your message.	Content that pushes the purchase decision. Positioning your superiority to competitors, inspiring confidence, and challenging assumptions. E.g. "easily digestible infographics, case studies, or pitch decks."	Engage followers with prospect converting content. Providing them with content to make an informed purchase decision. E.g. Posts of "customer stories, demonstrations, and webinars."

Table 6.7.1 – A summarised view of lead techniques by funnel position.

7.7 Adapt To Survive

As we have discussed at length, customer behaviour is an evolving creature. Companies that understand, anticipate, and deliver with this evolution in mind are the ones that are driving growth. Consider the increase in data being generated through the buyer journey via switching apps, sites, and devices, coupled with customers moving increasingly faster, expecting real-time assistance and immediate response to their needs.

Give careful consideration to the changes and innovations we have discussed. Where appropriate and relevant, adopt the model, techniques, and tools we have outlined to fit your sales funnel structure. Identify clear business objectives, align your funnel and marketing strategy accordingly. Measure, analyse, and experiment. Metrics and data are key, but not the be-all and end-all. Consider those traditional business measures such as profit, revenue, and human behaviour. But most of all, keep abreast of the changes and innovations taking place in the digital marketing space that impact your funnel. Take AI as an example. Whilst it is arguably costly to enter, it is increasingly becoming accessible in many ways, such as for Email and Chatbots. Being kept informed of what new software tools and services are making themselves available in this space is paramount to being on par, and if not, ahead of your online competitors. Join industry social media groups, blogs, and communities. Whilst you may be inundated with a great deal more email, every so often you will come across a nugget of information that may lead to game-changing conversions. Also you will be receiving on-going advice, learning best practices, and seeing examples of what successful enterprises are doing.

Finally, start small. Consider vague goals such as:

> "We need to increase traffic!"
>
> "We should focus on increasing conversions!"
>
> "We want to increase our social media presence!"

Clearly establish what you want to achieve, and when you want to achieve it. Then identify both short and long-term marketing strategies that are aligned with your objectives, leading to greater clarity when it comes to defining your sales funnel. Measure, track those KPI's, analyse, adapt, and refine. Learn to outshine your competitors by simply offering more value than they do. Use their successful strategies to create industry-leading content that's both uniquely you and uniquely valuable. Offer rich value and focus on the customer experience. Adapting to this approach will steer you towards realising growth, on which you build that business empire.

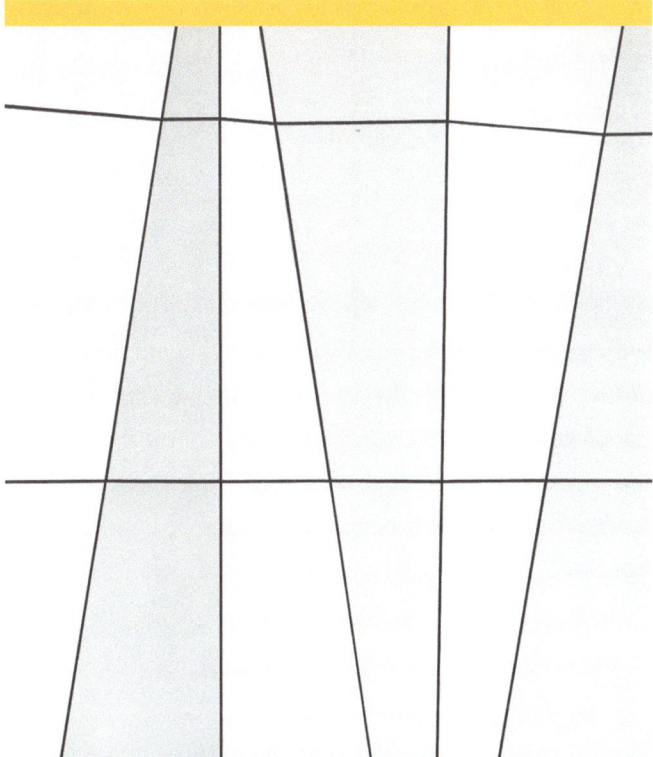

8.0 SALES FUNNEL SOFTWARE

> " **understand how to appropriate tools and services that will effectively sell your product and services.**"

It is estimated that 96% of visitors to your website are just window shopping, not quite in that "ready to purchase" frame of mind. With a little persuasion, they may hand over their contact information in exchange for content like newsletters, voucher codes, or guides. According to online sales funnel research, you have approximately 8 to 10 seconds to persuade them to stick around. To accomplish this, your sales funnel and marketing need to be up to par, as these ensure a consistent flow of prospects, which is the bedrock of customer growth.

According to Forbes, 80% of tech start-ups fail within their first 18 months. To increase your chances for online success, understand how to appropriate tools and services that will effectively sell your product and services. Those that make use of the concepts outlined in this book, giving you a head start with pre-defined funnels, metrics, and design content. There are several such available tools that can help you to build functional sales funnels but also providing pre-built templates for lead magnets for webinars, newsletter, and online courses. The beauty of all this is that they come packed with tools requiring no code or technical expertise and some, with clean design work. You just need a willingness to learn and jump right in.

Google Analytics

Google Analytics is probably the most prominent web analytical tool available. It offers a free service model that allows you to perform an in-depth analysis of website visits. It is a behemoth in terms of metrics, and the staple of web analytics for millions of sites worldwide.

Pros:
- Freely available and very well supported.
- Abundant ways to measure User Acquisition and User Behaviour data.
- Creates custom reports.
- Quick, simple funnel visualisation tool and analysis.
- Ideal for top of funnel analysis.
- Knowledge academy with extensive free online courses and certification.
- Optimised for mobile performance metrics.
- Creates custom goals to track e-commerce objectives.
- Strong integration with Google paid campaign tracking (PPC).
- Keyword analysis.

Cons:
- Basic funnel, not ideal for deep dive and optimisation.
- No in-depth analysis of "middle" journey, i.e., detailed visitor interaction.
- Lacking a complete behaviour analysis through the entire funnel.
- Free version suits small businesses, but the premium version is too expensive.
- Lacking big picture market reports.

Find out more: https://support.google.com/analytics/answer/1008015?hl=en

Oribi

Oribi is an all-in-one marketing analytics tool, catering for all business sizes, with easy to use dashboards and website statistics. It allows users to track goals and measure site activity. Their funnel features allow you to optimise your conversions by analysing what works and how to drive more conversions.

Pros:
- Simplicity is their main selling point.
- Great user experience ratings.
- Clear concise analytical presentation of data.
- Strong funnel visualisation and correlation features.
- Integration with multiples channels to source data from various streams.
- In-depth visitor behaviour analysis.
- Custom well-presented reports with automated sharing.
- Marketing attribution – uncover all touchpoints leading to conversion.
- User-friendly and actionable insights.

Cons:
- High start-up price, no free trial period.
- Out of reach for most start-ups.
- More emphasis on look and feel, rather than substance.

Find out more: https://oribi.io

Kartra

Founded by two reputable digital marketers in 2017, the original aim of this funnel building software was to replace the need to integrate with other subscription software. Instead, it provides a one shop tech solution, enabling the user to get anything up and running to cater for all their online selling needs.

Pros:
- Ready-made funnel templates that are easily edited.
- Create landing and sales pages easily with a drag and drop editor.
- In-built ticket support and customer management tool for your customers.
- Host and display videos, easily track video engagement.
- Automated sales-driven campaigns with an in-built auto responder.
- Behavioural adaptive marketing providing a customised and personalised experience for each customer.
- Payment gateway integration is in-built. Easy checkout services.
- Free trial period and reasonable entry price, $99/month.

Cons:
- Cost easily adds up as more funnels and features are added.
- The greater the traffic, the increase in the cost.
- Relatively new software, risking bugs and downtime during service maintenance.

Find out more: https://kartra.com

CHAPTER 8.0 SALES FUNNEL SOFTWARE

ClickFunnels

ClickFunnels is probably the most popular sales funnel building tool. It does everything from build landing and sales pages to online courses, create webinars, manage affiliates, and write sales scripts. Also, it teaches you about closing sales, leads and building email lists.

Pros:
- All-in-one funnel building tool. No plugins are required.
- Pre-built funnel templates that convert.
- Drag and drop sales funnel building.
- Affiliate management software.
- Email funnel follow-up, SMS sending, and Facebook automation.
- Good community support (220,000 Facebook members).
- Inbuilt automation for follow-up funnels.
- Reasonably priced – entry, $97/month.

Cons:
- Reports of email service going to spam.
- Limited customisation of pages. Template driven, not page.
- Poor customer service feedback.

Find out more: https://clickfunnels.com

GetResponse

GetResponse is primarily an email marketing platform, enabling the creation of marketing lists for prospects, partners, and clients. You can develop those relationships as a basis to drive your product selling. It lets you build landing pages, funnel conversions, sign-up forms, and webinars.

Pros:
- Dedicated email marketing tools for advanced email marketing automation.
- A ready-to-go sales funnel for generating traffic, sign-ups, and conversion.
- Customisable landing pages with a drag and drop editor.
- An e-commerce store where you can sell your physical products.
- Support for paid ads, such as Facebook.
- Team management and CRM.
- Very reasonable pricing, entry-level as low as $15/month.
- Ability to host webinars and perform split testing.

Cons:
- Very limited number of page templates and funnels.
- Poor page builder user interface.
- Only one funnel template on the cheapest plan.

Find out more: https://getresponse.com

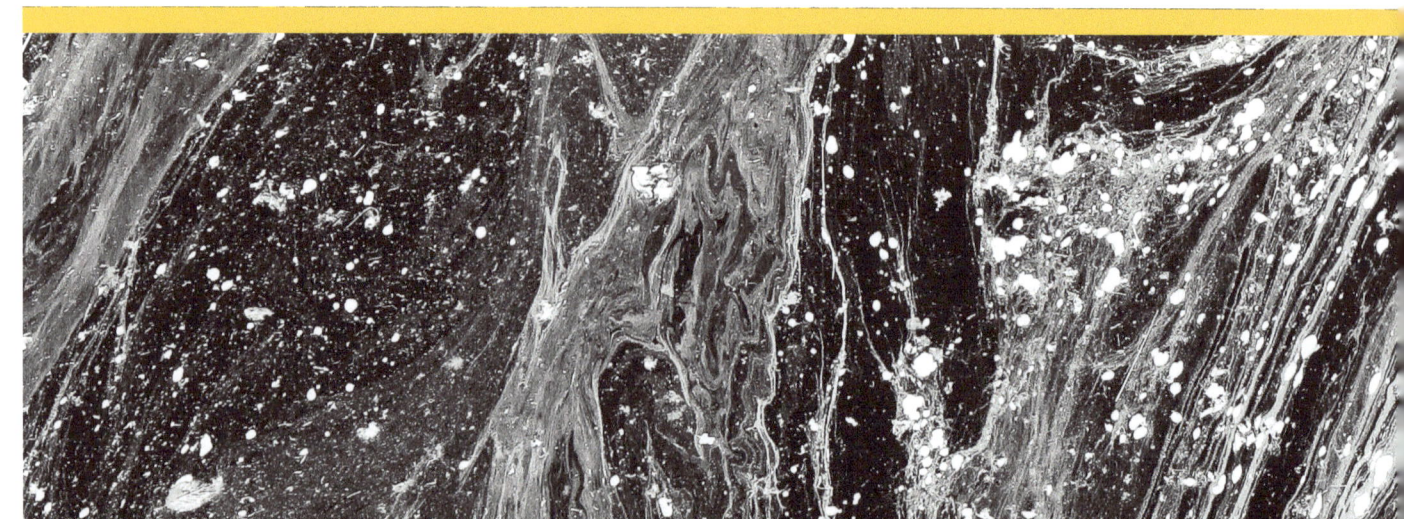

GrooveFunnels

A new player on the scene, it is a multifaceted page and funnel building platform that incorporates numerous tools for creating content, managing conversions, and marketing. The program is applicable for beginner and established marketers alike, with an unlimited lifetime free plan.

Pros:
- Easy-to-use funnel and webpage builder with easy drag-and-drop interface.
- Integrated payment gateways for e-commerce.
- Inbuilt email marketing services and CRM platform.
- An affiliate management programme.
- Helps you quickly host and create membership sites
- SEO optimized blog page templates.
- E-commerce and drop-shipping platform.
- Extremely attractive pricing for beginners and small businesses.

Cons:
- New to the market, BETA still in test, expect bugs.
- Complex and steep learning curve.
- Some of its tools being promoted are still not available.

Find out more: https://groovefunnels.com

Kajabi

Kajabi is one of the leading sales funnel platforms, especially for those marketing online courses. It has an all-on-one platform to bring courses and products to market, and a good selection of templates catering for landing pages, sales pages, webinar pages, and more.

Pros:
- Quick creation of pages, memberships, and funnels.
- Create marketing and email campaigns simply and quickly with a few clicks.
- Boost sales with one-click upsells and customisable checkouts.
- Reasonable entry price point at $119/month.
- Mature product, therefore well-supported and stable.
- Ideal for selling online courses.
- Built-in integration for selling via webinars.
- 24/7 support.
- 14 day free trial.

Cons:
- One of the more expensive solutions if you are looking to upgrade services.
- Not the most intuitive of editors.
- Limited third party integration.

Find out more: https://kajabi.com

Thrive Themes

It is a powerful sales funnel solution geared for WordPress creators. The program hosts a suite of WordPress website tools, conversion optimised plugins, and themes and was created to make selling, capturing leads, and driving meaningful business results for WordPress sites easy.

Pros:
- Easy and quick website development.
- Lead generation tools.
- Optimising tools that enable A/B testing.
- Very competitively priced $19/month.
- Industry funnel leader for WordPress websites.

Cons:
- Reportedly poor customer support.
- Difficult to use due to its close affiliation with WordPress.

Find out more: https://thrivethemes.com

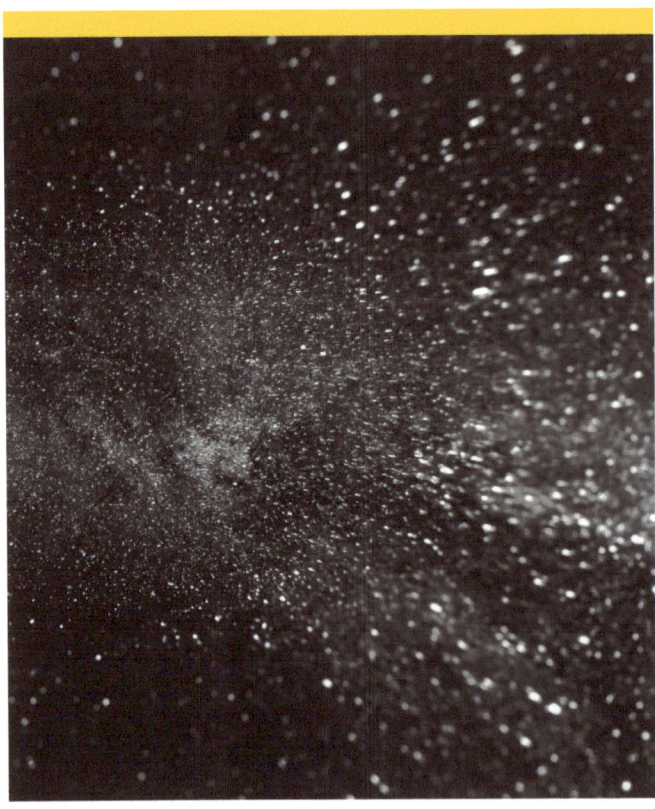

Keap

Previously known as Infusionsoft, which was founded in 2001, the primary focus of this platform is towards small businesses. It has solid email marketing solution, customer relationship management (CRM), and marketing automation functionality in one simple interface.

Pros:
- Saves small businesses on complicated data entry and messy marketing information systems.
- Lots of resources for the first-time user, as well as coaching.
- Reasonably priced for small business $79/month.
- Close integration of CRM and email marketing.
- 14-day free trial.
- Creates automated sales and marketing with marketing workflows.
- Strong funnel automation features.

Cons:
- Poor customer service feedback.
- Steep learning curve.
- Limited template options.

Find out more: https://keap.com

Finding the right sales funnel software for your business will depend on where you are in your business journey. At the very least, consider your budget, business goals, and marketing strategy. Review the features and plans on offer and develop a shortlist. The good thing is that most of these tools offer free trial periods. Use that time to become familiar with the software, until you find something that resonates with your business objectives and model. Remember, there will always be a new and shiny piece of software you can try. But no tool will solve the biggest problem of all – getting started!

9.0 WRAP UP

Your customers now expect you and your business to treat them as individuals and not as statistics. The capabilities of appropriate and personalized campaigns are colossal, and that is a fact well-known to your customers. So, as more businesses improve upon their marketing techniques and customer satisfaction processes, they raise the bar for those who do not.

This demonstrates that ultimately, the purpose of marketing is to attain customer satisfaction. When used in the way it is intended to, the sales and marketing funnel are powerful tools that can drive the future of your business in positive directions. The cornerstone of your sales and marketing strategy, dictating how to accommodate your customer needs and in constant state of flux through continuous refinement.

Technology is the basis of the online sales funnel. Recall the evolution from the AIDA model to a non-linear sales one. Technology will continue to transform, and you must stay informed. Amongst areas looking to be the most progressive are digital trends in email marketing, AI automation, and social media. Invest time and effort in a sales funnel that is flexible, allowing you to easily adopt these changes and be prepared for the innovation that will no doubt surface in the coming years.

Operate on the basis that your customers and their satisfaction are the ultimate end game so that you can kick-start the kind of business growth that hitherto has been impossible.

> "The modern customer demands to be treated as an individual, for their digital experiences and communications to be personalized and highly-relevant, and catered to match their specific needs, interests, and preferences. And while customer expectations are increasingly reaching all-time highs, their patience and tolerance for sub-par experiences are at all-time lows. As a customer, if you don't give me the quality experience I expect, exactly what I want, how, when, and where I want to experience it, I'll simply get it from someone else who will."

Gary DeAsi, Marketing Director, Pointilist.

10.0 **APPENDICES**

Appendix I **Funnel Models**

- Linear Funnel – Are conducive to the traditional customer lifecycle where the user moves from the top of the funnel (awareness) to the bottom (purchase) progressively and predictably.

- Non-Linear Funnel – User moves from top to bottom in a progressive but unpredictable manner.

  - Hourglass Funnel – Consists of up to 10 steps, a detailed approach stressing the importance of cultivating and sustaining relationships with customers.

  - Looping Funnel- A flexible and less organized funnel, featuring 6 stages, allowing every user to have their own distinct buyer's journey.

  - Micro-Moment Funnel – A funnel that focuses on the impetus that drives a prospect; want-to-know, want-to-do, want-to-buy, and want-to-go.

CHAPTER 10.0 APPENDICES   71

Appendix II **Funnel Objectives**

Classification	Objective	Description	Example	Ideal For
Sales	e-Commerce	For selling products and services online.	Landing page > Catalogue Page > Product Page > Add To Cart > Upsell > Checkout > Thank You Page	Online retail marketplace.
Marketing	Newsletter	For generating increased subscriptions to blogs or newsletters.	Social Media Content > CTA > Landing Page > Newsletter Registration > Email List > Email Nurturing	Media outlets, publications, communities.
Marketing	Email Marketing	Nurture audience via an automated email sequence to purchase products and services.	Lead magnet > Register > Landing page > Staggered Email Nurture Sequence > Sales Page > Product Page > Cart > Checkout > Thank You page.	Generating email subscribers for any business.
Marketing	Membership	For generating subscription members to your business, club, group, or society.	Organic Search > Landing Page > CTA > Download Free eBook > Register Subscription > Thank You Page > Welcome Email	Clubs, societies, groups.
Marketing	Affiliate Management	Created in conjunction with affiliate marketing efforts, or for promoting a product that marketers don't own.	PPC ad > Landing Page > CTA > Registered Email > Product Promotional Email > Sales Page > Cart > Checkout > Thank You Page	Digital marketers on affiliate programmes.

CHAPTER 10.0 APPENDICES

Appendix III Common & Successful Funnel Types

Classification	Category	How It Works	Example	Ideal For
Marketing	Lead Generation	Use a lead magnet to complete an opt-in form. Followed up by auto-responder email sequence, promoting product or service.	Social Ad > Landing Page > Email Opt-In > Automated Emails > Sales Page > Payment Page > Upsell Page > Thank You Page	Building leads, email lists, grow audience, acquire targeted leads ahead of a launch.
Marketing	Self-Liquidating Offer	Offering something cheap and accessible.	Paid ad > Landing page > Tripwire (sell something for really cheap) > Upsell #1 > Upsell #2	Liquidating ad costs, generate leads, build email lists, and eventually upsells.
Marketing	Organic Content Marketing	Using Google SEO and/or social media content to generate lead traffic to the funnel.	Blog post > CTA > Landing Page > Opt-In Form > Thank You Page > Email Sequence > Sales page > Upsell	Wide variety of products and services.
Sales	Welcome, Nurture & Sales Sequence	Send a new signed-up lead a welcome email, followed by nurturing emails sequence promoting your products.	Sign-up > Welcome Email > Nurturing Email Sequence > Selling Email Sequence > Sales Page > Cart > Checkout	Variety of products across price range and types.
Sales	Exploratory Call	Contact signed-up lead, immediately book a sales appointment or direct them to the sales page.	Sign-up > Auto responder Call Scheduler > Booking > Discovery Call > Sales page > Cart > Checkout	Qualified leads and high ticket items.

Appendix IV Funnel Categories

Classification	Category	How It Works	Example	Ideal For
Sales	Lead Magnet & Email	Nurture audience via an automated email sequence before pitching them a product after a few days.	*Lead magnet landing page > Email nurture sequence > Buy product > Upsell*	Low-ticket products using email services.
Sales	Cross-sell	Prospect in the process of purchasing a product, offer related product before checkout.	*Sales page > You Might Also Like Page > Add To Cart > Checkout > Thank You Page.*	All types of products.
Sales	Service Upsell	Get the prospect to buy an introductory product offer, then upsell them on a service that compliments the product.	*Sales page > Cart > You Might Want To Add? > Checkout > Thank You page.*	Products that you can upsell with a coaching package or related service.
Sales	Automated Webinar	Sell products or services through a live or recorded webinar.	*Landing Page > Register for Webinar > Booking > Live Webinar > Product Page > Add To Cart > Checkout > Thank You Email*	High-end products and services.
Sales	Referral	Prospect becomes a customer, try to indoctrinate them into becoming an affiliate by offering a referral incentive.	*Sign Up > Referral Code Redeemed > Purchase Service With Discount > Thank You page.*	Subscription-based services such as Dropbox or Netflix.
Marketing	High-End Client	Talk to a real person first, before asking them to spend money online.	*Service page > Page with a pre-qualifying questionnaire (for qualified leads) > Book Call > Free call > Register client > Thank You Email*	Creating qualified leads. Premium programs e.g., coaching packages, done-for-you services.

Classification	Category	How It Works	Example	Ideal For
Marketing	Affiliate	Collect email address, educate them about an affiliate product, follow-up through email, educate them further, pitch, and sell.	Relevant freebie > Thank you page with CTA to affiliate product > Email nurture sequence educating + adding value > soft-selling the affiliate product	Affiliate marketers.- Online entrepreneurs that do not have their products to sell.
Marketing	Free + Shipping	Offer product for free, just pay for shipping.	Lead magnet landing page > Free Product Page > Add To Cart > Upsell#1 > Upsell#2	Low-cost physical items like books. Generating leads for upsell.
Marketing	Challenge	Hold a 5 to 7-day challenge, e.g. 6-day weight loss contest.	Lead magnet landing Page > Sign-Up > Start Challenge > Product Page > Add To Cart > Upsell > Checkout	Health and wellbeing products and services.
Marketing	Free Sample	Give away a free sample of the product as a lead magnet. Follow up with email sequence.	Landing Page> Register Form > Automated Email Sequence > Sales Page > Upsell	Books, wellness products, and low-ticket consumables.
Marketing	Limited Time Product Launch	Create anticipation before people can buy a product or service; "sign-up before offer closes."	Landing Page > Register > Automated Emails > Sales Page > Launch Page > Add To Cart > Payment Page > Thank you page	Limited edition or information products.
Marketing	Free Consultation	Get visitors to speak directly with businesses about their products and services. Follow up with email.	Landing Page > Register > Consultation > Automated Emails > Sales Page > Payment Page > Thank you page	Information products or services. Multiple component and high-ticket items.

CHAPTER 10.0 APPENDICES

Appendix V Real-World Successful Funnels

Objective/ Category	Company	How It Works?	Why It Works?
- Subscription - Free Sample	**Netflix** Video streaming service.	Landing page with free trial > Pricing Page > Personalisation Page > Sign-Up > Payment Information > Content Home Page	- Clean simple user experience - Clear risk reversal offer – cancel anytime, No contract - FAQ's easily accessible and displayed. - Very end consumer focussed. - Strong emphasis on security. - Strong brand awareness.
- Email Marketing - Lead Magnet & Email	**Groupon** Digital coupon provider.	Direct/Ads/Affiliates/…> Landing Page > Sign-Up > Register > Latest Dewal Content Page	- Clear and prominent email opt-in on the landing page. - Clear CTA. - Strong incentives for sign-up (up to 70% on restaurants, spa, deals, etc.). - Tailored follow-up offers. - No free trials, not required. - Effectively a giant email list
- E-commerce - Challenge	**Annemarie** Skincare brand.	Social Media Content > Quiz Lead Magnet > Opt-In > Free Offers > Sales Page > Cart > Checkout > Thank You Page	- Strong social media presence driving traffic. - Clear "Quiz" Software CTA on most popular social media pages. - Incentives for completing quiz, e.g. $10 coupon. - Immediate use of incentives post quiz, directed to Sales pages. - Clear reviews, featured items, and samples to encourage sales.
- E-commerce - Lead Magnet	**Crazy Egg** Website optimisation tool.	Blog Post > CTA > Free Trial Sign-Up Page > Landing Page > Free Heatmap Sign-Up > Sales Pages > Cart > Checkout > Thank You Page	- Rich keyword featured blog - Blog sharing to email subscribers and social media influencers. - Various CTA's in every blog post. Including a 30 day free trial. - Landing page offers free website review - Clear persuasive copy to simply enter URL. - Social proof and thorough FAQ section.
- Email Marketing - E-commerce - Lead Magnet & Email	**Mixergy** Interview and course selling.	Google SEO > Landing page > CTA > Opt-In > Video Link Email > Landing Page > CTA > Premium Content Page > Cart > Checkout > Thank You Page	- Clear, immediate CTA for access to interviews in exchange for email. - Persuasive emails pushing premium content. - Premium content only available to registered email subscribers. - Registered members made to feel special. - Multiple CTA's on Landing Page promoting most recent interviews and courses. - One-click checkout and payment form. - Clear and concise copy on landing page.

Objective/ Category	Company	How It Works?	Why It Works?
■ Email Marketing ■ Free Sample	**Mailchimp** Email marketing tool.	*Organic/Blogs > Landing Page > Price/Features Page > Free Plan Sign-Up > Opt-In Form > Product Pages.*	■ Free plan ■ Strong brand awareness, through viral loop with a "Powered By Mailchimp" footer on all client, sent emails. ■ Landing page copy emphasises identity, free and self-expression. ■ Free advertising through millions of people using their service and indirectly promoting their products. Great example of social proof. ■ Simplicity of pricing plans. ■ Aspirational marketing copy, instead of hard-sell.
■ E-Commerce ■ Self-Liquidating Offer	**Drift** Live chat service.	*Blog/Organic/Affiliates > Landing Page > Pricing Page > Live Chat > Sign-Up > Free Service Plan*	■ Feature-rich blog. ■ Simple and effective landing page. ■ Interactive pricing page. ■ Easy, direct path to setup. ■ Sign-up, use service straightaway. ■ Free lifetime service. ■ Well thought out user experience.
■ Membership ■ Welcome, Nurture & Sales Sequence	**Mint** B2C financial services.	*Blog/Organic/Affiliates > Landing Page > Sign-Up Form > Opt-In > Service Pages.*	■ Completely free phone app. ■ Free sign-up. ■ "How It Works" page clearly displays services. ■ Personalised email credit card recommendations. ■ Simple, clear CTA ■ Trustworthy design. ■ Consistent visibility of sign-up button. ■ Complete transparency of exactly what you are signing up for.
■ Membership ■ Free Consultation	**Lawbite** Legal advice business	*Google SEO/Referrals > Book A Call CTA > Opt-In Form > Pricing Plans > Recommendations Page > Solicitor Website*	■ Clean website copy of services. ■ Strong CTA's for booking and joining. ■ Concise, simple sign-up for advice. ■ Clear and transparent "How It Works' copy. ■ Lifetime free plan ■ 15 min free consultation. ■ Immediate response with solicitor recommendations. ■ Good, clear options for getting in touch – call, live chat, or enquiry form.
■ Affiliate Management ■ Subscription ■ Affiliate	**CJ.com** Affiliate marketing program.	*Organic/Direct/Referrals > Landing page > Opt-In > Verification > Affiliate Resources*	■ Display of big brand client list. ■ Easy to navigate website. ■ Strong brand awareness. ■ Clear, minimal CTA's for both publish and advertiser sign-up. ■ Simple, effective display of persuasive, statistical information. ■ Strong advocacy of joining well-supported community. ■ Easy sign-up and getting started.

GLOSSARY

A/B Testing: A method of comparing two versions of a webpage or app against each other to determine which one performs better.

Action: Taking the next step towards purchasing a chosen product.

Advocates (brand): Someone who elevates your brand through word of mouth marketing, leaving positive reviews about your products, refers new customers and creates content on your behalf.

Affiliate: In retail, one company becomes affiliated with another to sell its products or services for a fee.

Affiliate Marketing: An arrangement between a seller and another business that gives a sales commission to the affiliate for promoting a product or line of products for the other company.

Awareness, Interest, Desire and Action (AIDA): Cognitive stages an individual goes through during the buying process for a product or service.

Artificial Intelligence (AI): Branch of computer science concerned with building smart machines capable of performing tasks that typically require human intelligence.

Back-end Sale: A product or service that you sell your customers after the initial sale.

Attribution: Which touchpoints, or marketing channels, receive credit for a conversion.

Awareness: The customer is aware of the existence of a product or service.

Banner Ad: Digital image advertising that is placed across various areas of a web page.

Beta (testing): Pre-release of product or service that is given out to a large group of users to try under real conditions.

Blog: Short for "web log", a blog is a web page or a website that is regularly updated with new written content. Ranging from a personal online diary to regular series of articles.

Bottleneck: Any part of the sales funnel where there is the least efficiency, and work, results, or leads get "stuck" or slowed down.

Bounce Rate: Refers to the percentage of visitors that leave your website after viewing only one page on your site.

Business To Business (B2B): Transaction or business conducted between one business and another, such as a wholesaler and retailer.

Business To Consumer (B2C): Process of selling products and services directly between a business and consumers who are the end-users of its products or services.

Campaign: A series of advertising messages that share a theme, and market a product or service. Can also refer to a comprehensive digital marketing strategy or project.

Channel (marketing): Any method or platform that's used to market a product or service to consumers. E.g., apps, blogs, websites.

Chatbot: A computer program that simulates and processes human conversation (written or spoken), allowing users to interact with digital devices as if they were communicating with a real person.

Churn: When existing customers stop doing business with you.

Cloud Computing: The delivery of computing services – including servers, storage, databases, networking, software, analytics and intelligence – over the Internet ("the cloud").

Click-Through-Rate (CTR): A measure of the number of clicks advertisers or emails receive as a percentage of the total number of impressions or campaign.

Content: Any form of online media that can be read, watched, or provides an interactive experience. Commonly refers to written materials, but also includes images and videos.

Content Marketing: A marketing technique of creating and distributing valuable, relevant and consistent content to attract and acquire a clearly defined audience.

Copy (marketing): Written material that encourages consumers to buy goods or services.

Consumer: A person who purchases goods and services for personal use.

Conversion: The completion of a predefined goal. Often used to track the number of site visitors that have been "converted" into paying customers, though sales is not necessarily the only metric; Other common goals are newsletter subscriptions and content downloads from a website.

Conversion Rate: Percentage of visitors to your website that complete a desired goal ("conversion") out of the total number of visitors.

Cookie: A small item of data sent from a website, that is stored on the user's device. Cookies help the user's device remember useful data like items in a shopping cart, which pages have already been visited or form field information.

Coupon Code: Digital discounts and promotions offered by retailers to current or prospective customers.

CTA (Call to Action): An element on a web page used to guide visitors towards a specific action or conversion. A CTA can be a clickable button, an image, or standard text. They typically use imperative verb phrases like: "Call Today" or "Buy Now".

Cross-selling: Sell related or complementary products to an existing customer.

Custom Form: Used to collect specific information from visitors on your website. E.g., buyer or contact information.

Customer Acquisition: Persuading consumers to purchase a company's products and/or services.

Customer Relationship Management (CRM): Technology used to manage interactions with customers and potential customers.

Cyber Crime: Online fraud, covers all crimes that: take place online; are committed using computers, or; are assisted by online technology.

Data Breach: Security incident where information is accessed, stolen, and used by a cybercriminal without authorization.

Demographic: Statistical characteristics of human populations (such as age or income) used especially to identify markets.

Desire: Aspiring to a particular brand or product.

Digital Marketing: Using the internet to reach consumers. Online strategies used in selling of products and services.

GLOSSARY

Drop Shipping: Retail fulfilment method where a store doesn't keep the products it sells in stock. Consequently, the seller doesn't have to handle the product directly.

eBook: Text presented in a format which allows it to be read on a computer or handheld device.

E-commerce: Stands for Electronic Commerce, the buying and selling of goods and services over the internet.

Email Marketing: The use of email as a marketing strategy to acquire sales, customers, or any other type of conversion.

Email Automation: Ability to send time or action triggered emails to subscribers with relevant information.

Engagement Rate: A measure of user interaction with a business or brand.

Entrance (funnel): Number of leads or potential customers that enter into your sales funnel in a certain period of time.

Eskimo: A member of an indigenous people inhabiting northern Canada, Alaska, Greenland, and eastern Siberia.

Flipbook (digital): An interactive e-book that looks just like a printed publication, with pages that can be flipped and turned.

Flipping The Funnel: Spending fewer resources on acquiring new customers and spending more on acknowledging and retaining current customers.

Forbes: Global media company, focusing on business, investing, technology, entrepreneurship, leadership, and lifestyle.

Fortune 500: One of the 500 largest companies in the United States

General Domestic Product (GDP): Monetary value of all finished goods and services made within a country during a specific period.

General Data Protection Regulation (GDPR): A regulation that requires businesses to protect the personal data and privacy of EU citizens for transactions that occur within EU member states.

Google Analytics: One of the most popular digital analytics software, allowing you to analyse in detail visitor interaction with your website.

Header: Refers to either the top portion of a webpage that typically contains the logo and menu, or the section of HTML in a website's code that contains important information about the site.

Heatmap: A graphical representation of data that uses a system of color-coding to represent different values.

Hourglass Funnel: A graphical representation that outlines the progression of potential customers in their buying journey; from the very first contact the customer has with the brand (Awareness), to nurturing the customer's interest (Education), confirming the customer's need (Validation), all the way to the purchase of the product or service (Purchase) and then through to Customer (Retention).

Impressions: A metric used to quantify the number of digital views or engagements of a piece of content, usually an advertisement, digital post, or a web page.

Influencer (social): People in social media who have built a reputation for their knowledge and expertise on a specific topic. Consequently having the power to affect the purchasing decisions of others.

GLOSSARY

Infographics: Visual representation of information or data, e.g. as a chart or diagram.

In-Process Conversion: The conversion rate of one stage of the funnel as a percentage of the next. E.g., 40% of visitors moved from Awareness to Interest.

Interest: Actively expressing an interest in a product group.

JavaScript: A scripting or programming language that allows you to implement complex features on web pages.

Keywords: Words or phrases that are used in search engines to search for online content.

Key Performance Indicator (KPI): A measurable value that demonstrates how effectively a business is achieving key business objectives.

Lagging Indicator: A performance indicator that is typically "output" oriented, easy to measure but hard to improve or influence. E.g., the number of accidents on a building site as a measure for performance safety.

Landing Page: An individual web page used specifically for marketing and advertising campaigns. Where a visitor "lands" from other channels such as email, ads or social media.

Lead: Contact with a potential customer, also known as a "prospect" or "sales contact".

Lead Generation: The process of generating leads by various means, e.g. calls, email, content etc.

Leading Indicator: A performance indicator that is typically "input" oriented, hard to measure and easy to influence. E.g., number of calls to a customer support desk.

Lead Magnet: An incentive that marketers offer to potential buyers in exchange for their email address or other contact information.

Linear Funnel: Conducive to the traditional customer lifecycle. The user moves from the top of the funnel (awareness) to the bottom (purchase) progressively and predictably.

Live Chat: Online customer service software with online chat, help desk software, and web analytics capabilities.

Looped Funnel: A sales funnel model that illustrates how consumers decide what they buy, and then continue to make purchases from a given company again in the future

Marketer: Is a person or a company creating a connection between a service or a product and the business.

Marketing Campaign: Promoting products and services through different types of media, such as television, radio, print, and online platforms.

Marketing Funnel: Describes your customer's journey from the initial stages to the purchasing stage and beyond. Mapping the route to conversion.

Merchant Account: Refers to an account where an ecommerce businesses can accept online payments.

Messenger Service: Any app that enables a private messaging function between two or more people.

Metric(s): Variety of measurements made on a given website in order to better track its performance and statistics.

GLOSSARY

Micro-moments Funnel: Building a sales funnel centred around Google inspired moments; "I want to know", "I want to go", "I want to do" and "I want to buy".

Newsletter: Giving those on your email list updates pertaining to your business, products, and services.

Non-Linear Funnel: A reinterpretation of the sales funnel where users move from top to bottom in a progressive but unpredictable manner.

Nurturing Email Sequence: A series of emails that are sent on the basis of a lead's behaviour, which deliver timely, targeted information that helps guide the lead through the buying process.

Omnichannel (marketing): Focuses on delivering a consistent, personalized experience for shoppers across all channels and devices.

Opt-In (marketing): Is a form of permission marketing in which there is a formal opt-in process for receiving follow-up communication, offers, etc.

Organic Traffic: Visitors coming from a search engine, such as Google or Bing.

Outcome Metrics: The specific data that you collect to assess the extent to which expected "outcomes" (e.g., changes in behaviours, attitudes, or knowledge) have been achieved.

Output Metrics: Your end goal, what makes your business succeed. E.g., revenue.

Overall Conversion: The ratio of people that went through the sales funnel to become buyers, against those that entered the funnel.

Parka: A type of coat, a well-insulated one that defies strong winds and cold, and it always has a hood that's (faux) fur-lined.

Payment Gateway: The gatekeeper of your customer payment data. Relays the information from you, the merchant, to the acquirer and the issuing bank using data encryption.

Payment Card Industry Security Standard (PCI DSS): A set of security standards designed to ensure that ALL companies that accept, process, store or transmit credit card information maintain a secure environment.

PayPal: Online financial service that allows you to pay for items using a secure internet account.

Pay Per Click (PPC): A model of internet marketing in which advertisers pay a fee each time one of their ads is clicked.

Persona (customer): A semi-fictional archetype that represents the key traits of a large segment of your audience, based on the data you've collected from user research and web analytics.

Personalised Email: When marketers use subscriber data within their email content to make the content feel tailor-made for the individual.

Pixel (JavaScript): Short snippet of JavaScript (code) that does something on your website. Often used to collect some information about the visitor to a website and their behaviour on the site.

Plugin: A software component that adds a specific feature to an existing software product.

Podcasts: A series of audio or video files that are syndicated over the Internet and stored on client computing devices for later playback.

Point Of Sale (POS): The place where your customer makes a payment for products or services at your store.

Prospect: A potential customer who has been deemed "qualified" by meeting certain criteria identified by the business.

GLOSSARY

Qualified Leads: prospective customer – who has been deemed ready for the sales team of your company to get in contact and close a sale.

Referral Program: A process in which you prime and reward customers for spreading the word about your product or service.

Retention (customer): The process of engaging existing customers to continue buying products or services from your business.

Revenue: The total amount of income generated by the sale of goods or services related to business's primary operations.

Retargeting: A form of online advertising that can help you keep your brand in front of bounced traffic after they leave your website.

Sales Cycle: A series of events or phases that occur during the selling of a product or service.

Sales Funnel: Each step that someone has to take in order to become your customer. A combination of marketing tactics utilized to generate traffic to your business and nurture them properly to become loyal customers who advocate for your business.

Software As A Service (SaaS): Also known as web-based software, on-demand software and hosted software. A delivery model in which software is licensed on a subscription basis and is centrally hosted.

Social Media: Websites and applications that enable users to create and share content or to participate in social networking.

Social Media Marketing: The use of social media platforms to connect with your audience to build your brand, increase sales, and drive website traffic.

Search Query: The term given for what is typed (words or phrases) by a user for performing searches in search engines such as Google.

Search Engine: Software system that is designed to carry out web searches.

Search Engine Marketing (SEM): The practice of marketing a business using paid advertisements that appear on search engine results pages (or SERPs).

Search Engine Optimization (SEO): The process and techniques by which a website ranks highly on search result pages. With a view to maximise visitors to the site organically.

Search Engine Results Page (SERP): Page featuring a list of results following a search query.

Secure Socket Layer (SSL): A security protocol that provides privacy, authentication, and integrity to Internet communications.

Segmentation (customer): The process of dividing customers into groups based on common characteristics so a business can market to each group effectively.

Self-Liquidating Offer: Allows you to create a cheaper version of what your main offer is about at the back of your sales funnel.

Shopping Cart: Piece of software on an online retailers site that facilitates the purchase of a product or service.

Small Medium Enterprise (SME): Small or medium-sized enterprise with fewer than 250 employees.

Sponsored Posts: A post to any community-driven notification-oriented website which is explicitly sponsored as an advertisement by a particular business for marketing purposes.

Testimonials (customer): are recommendations from satisfied buyers that affirm the value of a product or service.

Traffic Report (web): A report generated by web analytics software informing you of website activity.

Transaction Page: The goal of all your marketing efforts, the page where buyers enter their contact information and credit card number.

Transcript: the process of translating your video's audio or other audio recording into text.

Trigger Email: Those emails sent automatically based on pre-defined events or conditions met by an individual through certain behaviours, actions, or other signals.

Trustpilot: An open, online review platform where any consumer with a buying or service experience can review any company and any company can invite and respond to reviews for free.

Up-Selling: Convince the customer to buy a more expensive version of the product.

Unique Resource Locator (URL): The address of a resource such as a website address on the internet.

Velocity (funnel): Speed by which leads move through your sales funnel.

Web Analytics: A platform that allows webmasters to collate statistical information of website visits.

Webinar: A video workshop, lecture, or presentation hosted online using webinar software.

WordPress: A web publishing software you can use to create a websites. Includes flexible blogging and website content management system (CMS) for beginners.

Endnotes

[a] https://techgrabyte.com/economic-value-artificial-intelligence-growth-impact

[b] https://www.thinkwithgoogle.com/marketing-strategies/micro-moments/

We humbly request you leave an honest review on Amazon for this purchase, thank you.

www.ingramcontent.com/pod-product-compliance
Lightning Source LLC
Chambersburg PA
CBHW051157220526
45473CB00003B/811